Praise for

Let's Start Again

"Let's Start Again" is a call to the church to lead the way towards racial reconciliation in America. God's desire for his children to dwell together in unity is clear throughout scripture. It's time for His people to show the world what that can look like. Alex and Angela have laid down a challenge to those of us in the church to get busy being about our Father's business. Challenge accepted.
Mark Batterson
New York Times best selling author of *The Circle Maker*
Lead Pastor, National Community Church

You will appreciate the honesty and transparency with which Alex and Angela share their experiences living as a biracial couple in America. The USA's race relations problem isn't a skin color issue, but rather a spiritual battle between the powers of light and darkness in this world. This book is a challenge to the Church to take the lead in setting the narrative for racial reconciliation. Our God is in the reconciling business, and this book will help you see how you fit into His plan for racial reconciliation.
Pastor Herbert Cooper
Senior Pastor, People's Church
Author of *But God Changes Everything*

"Let's Start Again" *has been written by two very transparent people who live in a real world. I have had the unique privilege of observing them throughout their marriage and in each of their pastoral assignments demonstrating the principles and actions that they are proposing. As church leaders and mentors with a very prominent public presence, their voices speak with authenticity. They share their stories of helping bring diverse groups together to forge collaboration and establish racial reconciliation. This book is not an 'Idea of the Month.' Rather, it allows the reader to have a glimpse into the hearts and lives of Alex and Angela who believe very sincerely that the Church can have a fresh beginning of orchestrating racial harmony. They firmly believe and live by the conviction that 'By this all men will know that you are my disciples, if you love one another' (John 13:35 NIV). They believe that God can and will use the Church to accomplish what is desperately needed in our nation and around the world.*
Robert H. Spence
President Emeritus, Evangel University

Let's Start Again *offers a Gospel-centered take on America's current race struggle. Alex and Angela will challenge you to reframe your thinking about race relations as a spiritual battle rather than a man-to-man struggle. This battle can only truly be won through the reconciling power of Jesus Christ. You will come away from this book encouraged and ready to get in the fight!*
Pastor Rich Wilkerson Sr.
Senior Pastor, Trinity Church Miami

I have had the pleasure of knowing Alex and Angela since they were teenagers. I had the honor of officiating their wedding ceremony and knew then that God had plans to use them and their story to bring healing to hearts broken over the sin of racism. God has raised them up for such a time as this. We can all learn something about God's heart for racial reconciliation from the pages of Let's Start Again*!*
Reggie Dabbs
Motivational Speaker
Author of *Reggie: You Can't Change Your Past, But You Can Change Your Future and Just Keep Breathing*

The racial separation and sin in America just won't seem to go away. Alex and Angela Bryant struck a chord with nearly 40 million people with their viral video that cast the problem as something that can be overcome through love and unity. They have done it again with this book. In it, they share many personal experiences of living as a biracial family and offer valuable insights and helpful information to assist churches and community groups find their way through the sound bites that keep us divided. Let's Start Again *is not theory but a spiritual journey that I am pleased to endorse.*
Gary Grogan, aka Papa G
Legacy Pastor, Stone Creek Church, Urbana, IL

Alex and Angela Bryant have hit the hammer on the nail-head with Let's Start Again. *They are saying the things that you might be thinking (but have been afraid to say). Our country needs someone to address the race relations problem in America in a way that is in alignment with God's heart on the matter.* Let's Start Again *does just that.*
Dr. Alton Garrison
Executive Director, Acts 2 Journey Initiative

When we first meet someone, we automatically notice their gender, ethnicity, and age. These distinguishing factors are the very things we are tempted to discriminate on as well. Alex and Angela Bryant know firsthand the realities, tension, and racial biases present in America. Their book is a practical and powerful tool that will open eyes and hearts and will prayerfully start the dialogue necessary to close the racial divide in our nation.
Bishop Walter Harvey
President, National Black Fellowship, Assemblies of God

Let's Start Again
A Biracial Couple's View on Race, Racial Ignorance, and Racial Insensitivity

Published by Three Clicks Publishing
Springfield, MO

Let's Start Again
ISBN 978-1-7330962-5-6

Cover and interior design: Christy Demoff

Printed in the United States of America

12-142019 1

Let's Start Again

Acknowledgements

We would first and foremost like to thank God for considering us trustworthy enough to deliver this message to the world. We are both humbled and honored and plan to do everything within our power to be faithful to deliver the message of Love, Forgiveness, Unity, and Peace. We can all choose to live in the light.

In addition, there are a few key people who helped us turn the message into the book in your hand. We still can't believe it has really happened ourselves!

We want to thank Chris Thomas for helping us find our voice. For years you have been our editor and you have always encouraged us to keep writing. Thank you. Also, a big shout out to Amy as well.
Gary Grogan (Papa G), for over 30 years you have been a positive voice in our corner and have provided hours of mentoring, good advice and constructive feedback on this project. Thanks for helping us narrow the focus.

Kevin and KyAnne Weaver, you two were there for us when "Alex and Angie" were established. You believed in us, supported us, and now helped us produce this book for all the world to see. We are looking forward to many more projects in the future.

Sam Coryell, thanks for your friendship, the encouragement to write this book, and for helping make it happen! You da man!

Christy Demoff, from the very beginning, you "got us"! Thank you for lending your creativity to this project and for making it all come together.

Finally, to our kids and family, thank you for sharing life and memories and for giving us something to write about. You are our greatest blessings!

Word...

Contents

Foreword

When you know your purpose in life, and choose to fully embrace it, you will find yourself doing hard things in order to fulfill it. You will have hard conversations, you will address the elephant in the room, you will confront injustice and buck the status quo. Even if it makes you feel uncomfortable, you will take action because you realize that some things are too important to leave undone.

The 'racial tension' in our country is calling out for someone to address it. We don't want to be a 'racist' society. We don't want others to feel discriminated against or experience injustice just because they are a certain color. However, since we have not been able to come together and find common ground (a safe place that allows room for repentance, healing, forgiveness, love, unity and peace) this issue continues to plague our society.

We continue to see the ugly effects of 'racism' all around us in the forms of fear, hate, violence, and division. It's hard to know what to do. Thankfully, we know where to turn. As we direct our hearts, minds, and fortunes towards the Word of God, we will discover freedom and win liberty from the socially engineered and grossly deceptive concept of separate races in the human family.

The term "Racism" is rooted in a lie: that ethnically defined people groupings of human beings are somehow separate races. In Acts 17:26 we read that God has made of one blood all nations comprised of human beings to dwell on all the face of the earth.

All biblically and historically accurate accounts of the human family refer to us as nations, tongues, and tribes; not races.

Any language and definitions to the contrary are deceptive. Think about it. Why are we defining our brothers and sisters of blended ethnic origins as mixed? How often have we referred to children of obvious multi-ethnic origins as mixed? How often have we referred to ethnically blended marriages as mixed? Mixed with what? It's all human flesh and blood for God's sake; unless we are part Klingon or Endorian.

We are all ONE HUMAN RACE. Our skin color does not define our race; our One Blood does. We may be different ethnicities; our skin color may be different hues; our cultures may be different. But we are still just ONE RACE, HUMAN. 'Racism,' 'racial tension,' 'interracial,' 'race relations,' and the such are all human constructs that serve to divide us.

This socially engineered system defies religion, science, and biology. This macabre concept of separate races promulgates the lie of racism, that we humans are of different races. This is a lie that the enemy has been spreading for decades into centuries. We need to change our whole perspective and way of thinking and see each other as God sees us: as valuable, living children of God, created in His image as one human family.

"We must learn to live together as brothers [and sisters], or perish together as fools." – The Prophet Martin Luther King, Jr.

In the King Family tree, into which I was born, through the science of DNA matching, we have traced our ancestry to Africa, Ireland and Native America. So I ask you: what race am I? The obvious answer is human. So are you; human - if your blood is red.

"We all bleed the same." – President Donald J. Trump

The God of the universe, who creates ALL men and women in His likeness, wants the world to know that He has the answer to the problem.

Galatians 3:28 (NIV) states, "There is neither Jew nor Gentile, neither slave nor free, nor is there male and female, for you are all one in Christ Jesus." We are all one in Christ and yet our daily interactions often fail to reflect that truth. We have allowed the systems of this world to drive us to our separate corners and we live our lives in factions. Our enemy is quite adept at the divide and conquer strategy of warfare. Jesus himself left these words of instruction:

"By this everyone will know that you are my disciples, if you love one another" John 13:35 (NIV).

What message are we sending the watching world when it comes to how well we are loving each other? How well are our white brothers and sisters loving our black brothers and sisters and vice versa? Regardless of the reasons why we aren't doing a better job, I think we can all agree that the same God that reconciled you and me unto Himself can, and wants to, reconcile His followers with each other. God is a God of community and fellowship. Our enemy specializes in division and isolation.

All around our country, people are talking about 'race.' Whether it be face to face with a neighbor, posting about it on social media, or sitting around their dinner table in the privacy of their own home, they are talking about it. It's hard to ignore that there are a lot of opinions and dialogue being shared all around us about 'race,' 'racism,' 'racial injustice,' etc.

Politicians use this issue to try and get our votes or to dissuade us from voting for their opponents. The media continues to gain viewers and followers by bringing us polarizing stories that have a hint of 'racism,' realizing that we all have an insatiable desire to know more about the 'racial tension' in our country. There is a whole lot of talk with very little progress towards 'racial unity.'

As you read *Let's Start Again* you will gain fresh insight into why it's important to our Heavenly Father that we, His Church, get this 'race' thing figured out. It's been holding us back from our purpose for centuries. It is time for black, white, brown, yellow, and every other shade under the sun followers of Christ to stand united against our enemy and to show the world what love looks like. Then, we can offer the people in this love-starved world a better picture of what God's love can mean to them, and ultimately to introduce them to Him and welcome them into the family. We CAN fulfill our purpose as members of the human race.

Evangelist Alveda King

Let's Start Again

INTRODUCTION

A BIRACIAL COUPLE'S VIEW ON **RACE** **RACIAL IGNORANCE** **RACIAL INSENSITIVITY**

In July 2016, my family and I experienced something life-changing: we posted a video on Facebook that went viral. To date, the video has over 35 million views. Crazy! In addition, because of that video, we received about 5000 messages from people around the country and all over the world expressing how the video had touched their hearts. We never would have imagined that our family, from a small town in Missouri, would have touched the hearts of so many people. I don't consider myself a creative person, but that day I knew God was speaking directly to my heart and that our family had to share the message with the world. Here's our story.

On July 7, 2016, Micah Xavier Johnson ambushed and fired upon a group of police officers in Dallas, Texas, killing five officers and injuring nine others. Reportedly, he was angry over police shooting black men and stated that he wanted to kill white people, especially white police officers. The shooting happened at the end of a protest against the police killings of Alton Sterling in Baton Rouge, Louisiana, and Philando Castile from Falcon Heights, Minnesota, which had occurred in the preceding days.[1] That was a Thursday night. I remember hearing about these stories while I was out driving Uber™. My wife initially called to tell me what had happened. Then, as I picked up different riders throughout the night, I had a front row seat to hear many different people, from all walks of life, voice their thoughts on this incident. I found the perspectives of such dissimilar riders thought-provoking. The overwhelming consensus throughout the evening was that this was a senseless act of violence. No police officer should be targeted and murdered while trying to serve and protect. However, one or two riders had a different perspective. They felt the shootings were a natural consequence to the brutality that police officers were displaying to the black community, almost as if to say, "They had it coming!" This story was all over the radio and news. While driving that night, I had plenty of time to reflect on this tragic incident, and it weighed heavily on my heart.

The next morning, I had to take my oldest son to an appointment. While he was inside receiving physical therapy for a sports injury, I stayed in the car and scoured the internet for more information about the shooting the night before. As I learned more, my heart became more broken. I was extremely sad for the families of the fallen police officers. Their loved ones were never coming home again. I thought about my cousins who are police officers in Illinois. I remember talking to the wife of my cousin, Guy, and she told me that every time he put on his uniform and went to work, she was afraid he might not come home. That is a heavy burden to bear.

I also thought about the city of Dallas. Any event like that would divide the city for years, if not decades. The racial tension in America was widespread at this time; I wasn't sure Dallas was ready for what could come next. I had been living in St. Louis during the Mike Brown incident, which transpired in the suburb of Ferguson, Missouri. I ran an inner-city outreach ministry located just five miles from Ferguson. I was sitting in my office when I first heard about that police shooting and was one of the pastors who was asked to come and help intervene in an effort to keep peace on the streets of Ferguson. Days after the incident, I actually visited the spot where Mike Brown took his last breath. I met with police officers, protestors, and pastors to discuss how we could all work together to make sure protests remained peaceful. I visited the command center where the police officers staged their operations, and I met with Captain Ron Johnson of the Missouri Highway Patrol who led the police response. I saw firsthand how emotions ran high and how those emotions impacted the behavior of people (of all colors) toward others who didn't look like them.

My heart broke for our country. I kept asking myself, *How did it come to this*? Many Americans realized that racial tension was high at this time, and people put blame on different things: police brutality, political rhetoric, the criminal justice system, inner-city crime, then President Trump. As I sat in my car trying to figure out who I wanted to put the blame on, the Lord spoke to me, showing me that no one person was to blame. Rather, **we are all to blame**.

Our society has moved away from God's commandment to love one another, and as a result, we are experiencing an upswing in quarreling and blaming one another. This has to change! We need to start again and this time . . . let love lead the way.

At this point, allow me to rewind and let you in on how God had been preparing me for that July day in 2016. You see, a few weeks prior, my daughter had surgery to have her tonsils removed. Her recovery process included watching the movie "Annie" at least a dozen times (don't hate . . . it's actually a pretty good movie). Jamie Foxx can saaang! Not sing, but saaang! He's the kind of smooth brotha' who can not only act, but also captivate an audience by sitting down at a piano and serenading a crowd. I loved the soundtrack from the movie and listened to it on repeat for days. While I was in my car having this moment with the Lord, a song from the movie "Annie" came to mind. I played it. Then I played it again. Then I played it again. I sat in my car, praying, listening to this song, and thinking, as the tears kept flowing. The lyrics of that song kept playing through my mind . . .

"I want to start again, so I'll look within
Remember when I'd want in?
'Cause I don't know who I've become
But I will trust in it. I will trust in it
But today, I've got to make,

The best I can of it.
'Cause yesterday is dead and gone
And me along with it
I want to start again."

I began to wonder what it would look like if we, America, could all start again. What kind of country would we have? What changes would we make to right the wrongs of injustice, slavery, and racism? What would our country look like if Martin Luther King's dream had come to fruition? His dream of racial reconciliation. His dream of justice and equality for all people. His dream of a united country where little black boys and girls would hold hands with little white boys and girls. Was any of this possible? I didn't know then, and I still don't. But, is it worth dreaming about or striving for? I say yes. I knew that in order for any of this to come to pass, we would need God's help.

My son Trey finished his appointment, and we headed home. The whole time, I played this song on repeat and drove in silence while tears ran down my face. Trey didn't interrupt this moment with chatter. He could tell that something was going on inside of me, and he was sensitive to what he could see was happening. I'm certain that God spoke directly to that 15-year-old kid and told him to just be still. When I look back on that ride home, I'm thankful to have witnessed God bringing my son into the process with me.

When I arrived home, my wife, Angie, could tell something was on my heart. I told her what I was thinking about and that I had a message I had to write. She said she'd keep the kids out of my hair while I went downstairs to focus and work on writing down what God was telling me.

What happened next was as close to divine inspiration as I have ever experienced. I'd written many sermons at this point in my life. Some good, some not so good, and a few that I thought would have been worthy of preaching to an audience with Jesus in it. But this was divine inspiration like I'd never experienced it before. I grabbed a piece of paper and wrote a few simple phrases on the page. I was done in ten minutes. The Lord gave me exactly what to say, and all I had to do was write it down. I went back upstairs and shared with Ang what I had written. I told her I was going to make a video with note cards displaying the phrases I had written down. Then it got even cooler! It was as though God gave her the plans for what was to happen next. She had the rest of the details that would bring it all together; choosing the colors we wore, writing the note cards, including our kids, and the timing and staging of the video. Looking back, many of those details were mentioned in emails we received from people all over the country. As well, when we've had the chance to play the video in front of a live audience, they inevitably show their emotion as each child comes on the screen, ending with our youngest child, Katie, who happens to be our only girl. We truly believe that all of this was given to us by God and divinely used to relay a message He wants us all to hear.

That message is what this book is all about. I was given a vision that day for a new start. We believe God wants to use Christians to bring about racial unity. We will expand on this thought later in the book. In addition, He led us to the Scripture found in 1 John 1:5-7 (NIV): "*This is the message we have heard from him and declare to you: God is light; in him there is no darkness at all. If we claim to have fellowship with him and yet walk in the darkness, we lie and do not live out the truth. But if we walk in the light, as he is in the light, we have fellowship with one another, and the blood of Jesus, his Son, purifies us from all sin.*"

When examining the context of this passage, it's necessary to ask who the author was talking to at the time and what he meant. Then we should ask ourselves what it means for us today and how to apply the lesson to our lives. This message was given to followers of Jesus Christ: Christians. They were the ones who heard the messages about Jesus and His extraordinary love. The biblical author wrote this to Christians in the Early Church, and it still applies to us today. This is a timeless message that we all need to declare. God is light.

There is no darkness in Him at all. So, those of us who claim to be Christians should live in the light. His light!

God is calling us to live as children of the light, and He gives us ample instructions in the Book of Ephesians, chapters 4-6. This passage of Scripture gives us instructions about how to think and act. It includes instructions about speaking honestly and dealing with anger, about showing kindness and being cordial. We are reminded to be compassionate and to imitate God in the way we live our lives. We are exhorted to live a life that displays wisdom and to make the most of all opportunities we are given. When we make an effort to live as children of the light, when we apply this principle from God's Word to the racial divide in our country, we will be the ones to usher in racial unity in our country and around the world.

This message isn't new, and we don't claim to have dreamed it up. We take God's Word at face value and recognize that in presenting this message, we can impact the world for God's glory. We often wonder why God chose to use us to spread this message to the world – a biracial couple from a little town outside of Kansas City, Missouri. People often ask if it was our goal to make a viral video. It wasn't. We just knew that the Lord spoke clearly to us and we wanted to be obedient by delivering the message He gave us. Many people find our story fascinating and have asked to know more about us and about the story of the video. In this book, we will share many stories from our personal experiences and offer our perspective on race, racism, and race relations in our country. The goal is to be unified as Christian brothers and sisters so that we can advance God's kingdom without race issues distracting us, and share with the world that God loves them and sent His Son, Jesus, to die for them.

Who Am I? Alex

CHAPTER ONE

1

Who Am I? Alex

Alex Levine Bryant, Jr., was born in Fort Pierce, Florida, on February 26, 1972. My parents were two unmarried teenagers who both ended up dropping out of high school. My dad was Alex Levine Bryant, Sr., who was 15 years old at the time of my birth. My mother, Barbara Lavern Cox, was 16 when she got pregnant with me. After a few days in the hospital, I was taken home to my grandmother's house. Catherine Cox ("Cat" is what I called her) owned a small two-bedroom house on 15th Street in Fort Pierce. Although this house was small, it was filled with a lot of love – AND, a lot of people. One of the two bedrooms was occupied by my Aunt Kaye and her four kids, all of whom were older than me. My Uncle Joey usually slept on the couch in the living room. In the other bedroom, Cat and I shared a twin bed; my mom occupied the other twin bed most of the time. I say "most of the time" because there were many times when she was out "running the streets." At this point in her life, my mom was known for being young, fast, and free. When she was off "doing her thing," Uncle Joey would sleep in her bed in the room with Grandma Cat and me. My real dad (that's how I refer to him) did not live with us. In fact, he and I have never slept a night under the same roof. He also ran the streets, and still does. Although he frequented the streets of Fort Pierce, he actually lived a couple hours away in Pahokee, with his mom, my beloved grandmother, Naomi. I remember that she was extremely nice, had a big smile, and that she was a chain smoker. I didn't spend much time with her. She died while I was in high school.

Growing up, I spent time moving back and forth between Fort Pierce, Florida, and Macomb, Illinois. These two towns were completely different. Fort Pierce is a racially segregated town of about 45,000 people. When I was a kid, I could go weeks without seeing a white person. Macomb, on the other hand, a much smaller and predominantly white community, seemed to be more diverse. That's because Macomb was (and still is) a college town. Western Illinois University brought about 10,000 students to this small farm community, many of whom were minorities and international students. So, my world was a little confusing. Part of the time I saw black and white people interacting, but when I went back to Fort Pierce, I saw black people only.

Since there wasn't much interaction with white people, we only heard the stories from my aunt's interactions with them. She worked at a health clinic that primarily serviced black people, but every now and then a "cracker" would come in. That's what I remember my family and other people in town called white people–cracker. Until I moved to Macomb, I didn't know white people were referred to any other way. Macomb was different. No one called people crackers. In fact, we had white people coming and going in our house. My mom and stepdad were actually friends with them. They would hang out at our house, party, and have a good time together. All of the going back and forth, being exposed to such drastic extremes, and constant change made for a pretty unstable family life.

I can remember my earliest memory like it was yesterday. I was about three years old. I was sitting on my couch alone, in the middle of the night, crying for my mother to come back home. I don't remember if it had been a few days or a few weeks at that point, but it would be two years until I saw her again. Although that was nearly 45 years ago, the memory is still just as vivid, and the pain still stings. My story is like many other poor black kids raised by a grandmother.

The reason I was up that night, sitting on the couch, crying, in my tightie-whitie Fruit of the Loom underwear and undershirt, was because I was abandoned. Even though I was only three years old, I knew I was abandoned. Days earlier, while I was at preschool, my mom had taken all of her stuff and skipped town. She didn't say goodbye, didn't leave a note. When I returned home from school that day, all of my mom's stuff was gone. At first, they told me she was just out of town for a couple of days, but it didn't take me long to realize that she wasn't coming back. A little while earlier, she had met a boy who had traveled to Florida for spring break. When the time came for him to go home, she decided that she wanted to go back to Illinois with him. She wanted to start a new life. Apparently, the plan was supposed to be that she would send for me "in a couple of weeks, once she got established." A couple of weeks turned into a couple of years – two years before I would see her again. In the meantime, I finished preschool and started kindergarten living with and being reared by my grandmother and Aunt Kaye. It was hard. I remember feeling alone and unloved.

I grew cold and hard and bitter toward my mom and everyone else. I didn't trust people. Even as a kid, I developed the philosophy that "If you can't trust your own mom, you can't trust anyone." I held tightly to that philosophy for almost 20 years, until I experienced a life-altering encounter with my then – girlfriend (now wife) Angie. Ang was the first person with whom I let my guard down, and, as a result, she helped me heal. I will pick up that part of the story later.

After a couple of years of being absent, my mom showed up and wanted to take me to live with her (and her boyfriend) in Illinois. And so she did. We lived in the housing projects, in a three-bedroom house with his mother and her three other kids. I attended kindergarten there for part of the year, but the conditions were tough (and I missed my grandmother), so my mom sent me back to Florida to finish kindergarten. During the summer, she returned to Florida to take me back to Illinois to live with her and a new boyfriend. I remember hating this arrangement. I acted up and rebelled again until she sent me back to Florida to live with Cat. I finished first grade at Francis K. Sweet Elementary School in Fort Pierce. Then, just before I was supposed to start second grade in Florida with all my friends, mom showed up and took me back to Illinois to live with her once again. I remember her telling me over and over, “It’s just you and me, buddy; Cat ain’t gonna save you this time!”

Moving back to Illinois and away from Cat was devastating. I was angry at my mom for moving me away from the only family that I ever knew, sad that Cat wouldn’t be around to spoil me, and just downright mad that things were changing. Since I didn’t know how to process all this change, I acted out and started fights with people for no reason at all. I didn’t care enough to apply myself and ended up doing poorly in school. By the time I was in third grade, I was placed in special education. To numb the pain I felt on the inside, I fought all the time and acted like the typical bully. That’s when my mom decided to try something new. Although she didn’t go, she started making me go to church.

Every single Sunday, I would walk out of the projects and down the street to Mount Calvary Church of God in Christ where the faithful Sunday school teacher, Mother Coleman would meet me at the door and tell me the same thing. She’d say, “Baby, Mother Coleman loves you, and God loves you, and He has a plan for your life!” Every single Sunday, she’d tell me that same thing. Then she’d give me a candy bar if I memorized the memory verse, or she’d give me a quarter for learning the Books of the Bible or some other Sunday school lesson. Every week, without fail, Mother Coleman would greet me at the door with a big smile, give me a long loving hug, and tell me that she loved me. And she never failed to remind me that God loved me and He had a plan for my life. Somewhere along the line, I started to believe her. This was the beginning of my walk with Christ.

Jesus changed my life. Shortly after I got saved, my attitude and behavior changed, and I started singing in the church choir. Eventually my mom and sister started coming. A couple of years later, we switched to the Assemblies of God church in town, where we were afforded the opportunity for deeper discipleship and teaching.

Macomb Assembly of God is where I was formally introduced to Angie Chapin. Angie was the prettiest and most godly girl in that church of 400 people. Even though I was a high school student and in no position to be married, I remember thinking that I wanted to one day marry a girl like her. I suppose that in the back of my mind, I was thinking I wanted her, but in a darker shade–the black version of Angie. I wasn't opposed to marrying a white girl, but I hadn't given it much thought. I just always assumed I would marry a black girl. Except for a couple of uncles that I had on my step-dad's side of the family, everyone I knew married within their own race. That's just what we did back then. The unwritten rule is that it was best to marry within your race. We didn't even have to talk about it. It's just what people did.

Who am I?

Angie and I quickly developed a close friendship. We challenged, encouraged, and motivated each other to go deeper in our walk with the Lord. When I left Macomb to attend Evangel University, Angie stayed in town to attend Western Illinois University, and yet we remained close friends.

However, our lives seemed to be moving in different directions. I dated other girls, and Angie got engaged to another guy. That relationship didn't work out, and they broke it off in the spring of 1992. That summer, I returned home from my sophomore year of college at Evangel University, and the sparks began to fly between the two of us. Our close friendship deepened, but we didn't get too serious because we knew I would be returning to college in just a couple months, and there would be a lot of miles between us.

All the while, God was working on my heart, bringing healing in the area of learning to trust people. I knew I was falling in love with this girl, but could I trust her? The following summer, Ang ended up moving to Springfield to attend the Assemblies of God Theological Seminary, and we quickly found ourselves in a committed relationship, talking about getting married. This scared me! My fears led me to look for an out before she hurt me like I believed everyone else had. Then, I found my reason to bolt.

I don't remember the details of the fight, but we were in the parking lot of the Battlefield Mall. I was ready to throw it all away and give up on any possible future with the girl of my dreams, all because I was afraid of being hurt. But in that moment I received deliverance and healing from the pain of abandonment and rejection. Ang took my face in her hands and looked me in the eyes and told me that she loved me, and she wasn't going anywhere. She asked me to trust her. It was the healing that I needed. I believed her and decided to trust her! God used Ang to help me see and realize how long I had been holding onto the fear of being abandoned and how deep my pain was.

I'd like to say I was completely restored at that moment; I wasn't. It has taken time and a lot of hard work to deal with past hurts. But, I'm healthy and on the journey of healing. Ang has helped me deal with the pain and feelings of resentment I held in my heart toward my mom and real dad. She's helped me turn those trials into my testimony. I have shared this testimony with people all over America and around the world. It's helped me connect with people and has caused them to open up their hearts to me. As a result, I've been able to present the gospel to them and have seen many accept Jesus as their personal Lord and Savior.

God picked up the broken pieces of my life and gave me beauty from the ashes. He gave me a fresh start. By His grace, and with the help of Ang, I've been able to start again. God has restored my relationship with my mom and dad. Shortly after I became a Christian, my mom started attending church and dedicated her life to God. He radically changed her life and restored her hope. She is one of the godliest women I know, and she is definitely my biggest prayer warrior. What the devil meant for harm, God used for His good. I'm a living witness that God can and will use anyone. I've learned that I don't have to repeat the mistakes of the past. I do my best to try to learn from the mistakes of others so I can be a wise person. Ang and I have been married 24 years, and we have five children. I strive to be the father to them that I never had. It's my goal to be the best dad possible and to be engaged and involved in their lives. At the same time, God has called Ang and me into full-time ministry. We know it is our mission to go (wherever God calls us) to make disciples. We use all of our talent, abilities, and resources to do just that. God has been very good to us, and we are attempting to follow Him with all of our heart, mind, soul, and strength as we travel on the journey of chasing after Him!

I'm thankful for the fresh new start I have been given. Since then, God has placed a call on our lives, and He has given us a vision and purpose for our lives and ministry together. This was revealed to us clearly while seeking the Lord at a conference in Denver, Colorado. Then and there, God offered us a glimpse of how we were to be used by Him. He clearly called us to be unifiers.

CHAPTER TWO

Who Am I? Angie

2

Who Am I? Angie

Who am I? Who are we? We are Alex and Angie. That's how our relationship began. We were friends from church for several years before we ever began dating. Once we started to date, we weren't comfortable calling it dating, so we just kept telling everyone that asked, "What are you guys?" that we were "Alex and Angie." Of course, it was obvious to anyone who wanted to see that we were dating, and, as Alex's mom put it, "Ya'll ain't fooling nobody but yourselves."

We aren't comfortable with labels. While we were trying to keep everything light and vague, it seemed that the rest of the world was insisting that we put ourselves in a box with just the right label. Thus, the question, "What are you guys?" There can be all kinds of reasons why people struggle to define their relationships. Let me share with you a few reasons why I did.

Black and white make gray. People aren't comfortable with gray. When Alex and I were "coming of age" in our teens in a small Midwestern town in Illinois, it would have been easy for people to say there were no race issues. There were no race riots, no calls for desegregation, no crosses being burned in people's yards. However, I've come to understand that people believed there were no race issues because black people and white people rarely interacted with one another. That fact alone was the problem. It's kind of like when your check engine light comes on, you go to a mechanic, and, after much time and money spent, he says: "Nothing's wrong." Am I the only person who feels that the check engine light being on (for no good reason) is a problem? Can you see where I'm going with this? The fact that black people and white people rarely interacted with one another was the problem. Here came Alex and Angie into the mix, and we started interacting with one another . . . a lot. That lit up the check engine light for our friends and family like the sky on the Fourth of July. The check engine light came on, but nothing was really wrong. Both Alex and I, along with our friends and family, had some serious investigating to do in order to understand all the gray taking place in our world.

My dad, who is now ninety years old, was born in 1929 to a factory worker in Chicago who was married to a "Southern Belle" from Valdosta, Georgia. Grandma and Grandpa were approximately twenty years old when Dad was born; their births took place around 1909. The Emancipation Proclamation was issued on January 1, 1863, less than fifty years before my grandma was born. I've been told that I have relatives who fought on both sides of the Civil War and that my great-great-grandparents owned slaves. That's pretty recent history in the big scheme of things. Grandma's worldview was shaped by her Southern roots. When it came to black and white people mixing . . . there was no room for gray. It wasn't done.

My grandparents didn't stay in Chicago long. They left Chicago and settled in West Central Illinois as farmers. In this location, at this time, the idea of black people and white people interacting was a nonissue. That's because there were no black people to interact with.

In contrast, I grew up in the early 1970s. By this time, the Civil Rights Movement had happened. My dad's youngest siblings were attending state university, studying to become teachers. Dad was working in a factory, and he did interact with black people at work. I remember being aware that he had black friends when I was a little girl, and, as I grew older, this stood out to me as a sign that in my family people were not judged by the color of their skin but by the content of their character. It's interesting that I never heard those words until many years later, but the message was one I received as a child. I also received the truth of the message from the classic Sunday school song with the line that says, "Red and yellow, black and white, they are precious in His sight." Unfortunately, I also heard racist jokes and learned racial stereotypes from friends and family members. Because my family was always up for a good laugh, I assumed that the jokes and the stereotypical talk were all in good fun. I later realized that none of that would have been funny to our black friends and that my family would not have spoken that way around black friends. One particular family story came via my young aunts. The question was posed to Grandma, "What would happen if one of us brought home a black boyfriend from college?" Her response was, "Well, your children wouldn't be allowed to call me Grandma." There was no room for gray. Message heard loud and clear.

My mother is several years younger than my dad. She, too, grew up in West Central Illinois, amid cornfields and without interaction with black people. The common knowledge folklore was that if black people were passing through, they were not allowed to stay in Mom's hometown after dark. Mom's family was poor, and Grandpa had enough Native American in him that he looked the part. My mom felt and understood the pain of poverty and racial prejudice. My mom is just one of those "nice" people. You know what I mean - always considerate of other people's feelings (almost too much at times). Sorry, Mom! I knew in my heart that my mom would be kind and loving to any person she encountered; I just don't remember her encountering many black people in my early years. There was an occasional black family who attended our church. They had often come to town to work for the local university in some capacity, and they usually ended up leaving our church to attend services at "the black church" on the other side of town. Mom was always friendly and welcoming to those families. Again, I took away the message that we weren't judging by skin color.

Keeping my upbringing in mind, let's get back to the story of Alex and me. We just clicked. We had chemistry, and we had a love for God that kept us connected throughout high school and on into college, even though we were in different states. We spent a lot of time together, mostly at church events, and we toyed with the idea of dating when I was a senior in high school. It just wasn't the right time. The main reason it wasn't the right time then was because of the mixed messages I had received as a child: Black and white people are all the same in God's sight; judge people by their character, not their skin color - BUT, black and white people interacting is gray, and **we're not comfortable with gray!**

A few years passed. I was engaged to a sweet young man I had met at college. Alex had moved away to attend Evangel University in Springfield, Missouri, and we had kept our friendship alive through phone calls and during school breaks. In fact, Alex was going to be an usher in my wedding, since we needed an extra guy. Those plans changed! I got "dis-engaged," and Alex came home from college for the summer. He and I started interacting with each other again. . . .a lot. This is really when the pressure came on for us to answer, "What are you guys?" Things were looking awfully gray to our friends and family.

At this point I knew I had some serious decisions to make. I was falling in love with Alex, and yet I knew that if I did (and went on to marry him) I faced a very real chance my family might not accept that decision. As long as we were just friends, we didn't have any issues with others accepting our relationship. But, once we decided to start dating, attitudes changed. All of sudden, the check engine light came on. I tried to assure everyone there was no problem. But, just like when the mechanic assures us everything is fine with our car even though the check engine light is on, everyone was driving around with the sense that something was wrong and that the problem would rear its ugly head at any time. People gave their advice: Think of the kids; You won't be able to get good ministry jobs; What will Mr. and Mrs. So and So think? My Mom consulted one trusted spiritual advisor and came away with the message that although the Bible doesn't say there's anything wrong with biracial marriage, if it was his daughter. . . .he wouldn't want her to do it. The check engine light was on, and nothing was wrong! The problem itself was the unwritten rule that black and white people just aren't supposed to interact that much.

I remember being very disappointed in close family and friends and in church members who I believed had taught me to be open and loving toward all people, regardless of skin color or socioeconomic status. These people had taught me to judge by the content of a person's character, not by the color of his or her skin. Yet when I applied that standard to my potential husband, the truth about what people believed was clearly revealed. What most of my friends and family believed was that black people and white people are just not supposed to interact closely.

We have a choice to make. Do we drive around with the check engine light on and assure ourselves everything is fine? Or, do we get to work to solve the problem and get rid of that annoying check engine light? How do we change things so that black people and white people interacting doesn't set the alarms off in the first place?

I wrestled with my decision. I listened to the voices hinting that my family might cut me out of their lives if I chose to marry Alex. I sought out godly advice from church leaders who helped me to hear God's heart on this matter. I didn't want to dishonor my family, but neither did I want to dishonor Alex and our relationship simply because he was black, and I was white.

God has been faithful to help us walk out our relationship journey. Family relationships survived and are healthy now. In fact, sometimes, I think they like him more than they like me! We have seen God break down racial barriers in our own family. Alex is not the black son-in-law. He's just Alex, the son-in-law, the brother-in-law, the uncle. God is able to change hearts and minds; we should never doubt His ability to work!

One of the best examples of this kind of heart change happened to that "Southern Belle" grandmother of mine. Grandma never imagined she would accept a young black man into her family. But, God is able to do immeasurably more than all we ask or imagine Ephesians 3:20-21 (NIV).

Grandma was too frail to attend our wedding, but after the ceremony, Alex and I went to visit her in our wedding attire. She welcomed us with open arms. And, just two short years later. . . .Alex sang a beautiful hymn at her funeral.

Friends, we don't have nearly the amount of baggage to overcome that my grandmother did when she chose to start again. If she could do it, then so can you and I. Let's Start Again!

> *"Now to him who is able to do immeasurably more than all we ask or imagine, according to his power that is at work within us, to him be glory in the church and in Christ Jesus throughout all generations, forever and ever! Amen"* Ephesians 3:20-21 *(NIV).*

Who Are We?

CHAPTER THREE

3

Who Are We?

In 2005, at a pastors' meeting for our fellowship in Denver, Colorado, God downloaded His purpose for us, our marriage, and our family. We were listening to a message by Pastor Bryan Jarrett. He was sharing how the gospel needs to be shared from one generation to the next and how it takes cooperation and clear communication from all involved in the transition. He referenced Judges 2:10 and said that after one generation died, a generation grew up who didn't know God or the miracles that He had performed. The younger generation wasn't taught about God. They didn't learn history and didn't know their mission moving forward. They needed people who would bridge the gap and teach the younger generation.

When we attended this conference, we were in our early thirties. We were working as youth pastors and loved being around young people. We found we were in the middle of a few generations. We didn't fully belong to either generation. We loved young people and also appreciated being around older people, so we found ourselves in a unique position to relate either way.

Additionally, because we are a biracial couple, we have always felt comfortable around black people and white people. Then and there God solidified in our hearts that we were to be used to help bridge generations and bridge races. We hid this in our hearts and looked for ways to connect people.

The revelation we received in the service that night taught us to see race in a different light. We do our best to see people for who they are, not what race or ethnic group they belong to. We're not saying that we don't see race. I'm a large black man, and Ang is a small white woman. We've come to realize that race can describe us, but it does not define us. We will go into this in more detail later. We have become comfortable with acknowledging the differences between our races. We talk about it with each other, with our kids, and with our family and friends. We even joke about it. Admittedly, this makes some people uncomfortable, but we have to be able to speak about the elephant in the room. Humor is usually the best way to get the conversation going. In order to help bridge the gap between races, we all have to be more comfortable talking about race. This will lead to being more comfortable around people of other races. We must realize that even though we are different colors, shades, or ethnicities, we are all still part of the human race. And, we are all Americans. A house divided cannot stand.

When we posed the question, "Who are we becoming?" in the video, it was a challenge to introspection. The goal was to prompt people to look within themselves and examine their thoughts about race. We wanted them to ask themselves a couple of questions:

- What is my responsibility toward my fellow man?
- What message do I want to relay to my kids?

We received thousands of emails in response to our video. One of the main things people did was share pictures of their kids and families. We did not ask them to do this; it was their natural response. By seeing pictures of our family and us asking the question, "Who are we becoming?," people naturally thought about the future for their kids. It makes us realize that we are all connected. It's not hard to see that America is full of diversity. And that's a good thing. We can be proud of our heritage and where we came from and still be accepting of the fact that America is changing and we are becoming something other than what we were. It's no longer about me; it's about us. United we stand and divided we fall.

Once we realize this, we should begin to plan to leave a positive legacy for our loved ones. We must be considerate of who we are becoming for the sake of future generations. All of us have influence over someone. How are you using your influence to improve race relations in our country?

Our forefathers have struggled with race relations since the first white man stepped foot in North America. We need racial reconciliation. It is time to evaluate what we believe our response should be to the race relations problem permeating our nation. I imagine you are aware of this problem, since you have decided to purchase this book and have read thus far. The solution to a problem always begins by first acknowledging the existence of that problem. We have to acknowledge we have a race problem in America!

For many black and brown people in America, it's not hard to acknowledge this problem. Even today, I would dare say that most, if not all, minorities have personally experienced racism and/or prejudice, or at least know someone who has. Negative encounters with the police have been part of the status quo. My mom told me the story of an encounter that has stuck with her for many years. My stepfather and his brother were at a bar close to their house, near the "black" side of town. They were minding their own business when a couple of white men, who obviously had too much to drink, began to harass them for no good reason. My dad and his brother tried to ignore them at first, but it wasn't long before the N-word began to fly. That's when it all went down! The situation turned physical fairly quickly and one of the men ended up hitting my dad across the back with a baseball bat. This normally would be considered assault with a weapon. But not at that bar that night. Without really hearing both sides, the police ended up cuffing my dad and his brother and hauling them off to jail. They were the only two to be arrested that night. For years following the incident, my dad and my uncle, remained guarded and untrusting of police. A similar feeling could be said of most black people I knew growing up.

Who are we?

We have to begin by admitting a problem. A lot of white people can't fathom the reality that many black people live with on a regular basis. For me personally, I will admit that most of my experiences with police have been positive, but I've had a few occurrences that could raise eyebrows.

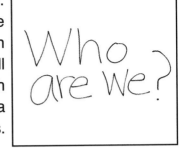

I remember one such time while I was attending college in Springfield, Missouri, there was a young white lady that I was seeing at the time. One night we visited a local spot out by the airport that many young people frequented for its romantic atmosphere. This particular spot was extremely close to a runway and the planes would fly low and close just before landing. Visitors would go there to park and usually sit on the trunk of their car and watch the planes come in and land. We pulled onto the gravel road that was about a football field long and quickly noticed that there were two other cars already there. One car was parked at the beginning and the other was at the far end, so I pulled in about halfway between them. We sat in the car and watched a few planes arrive and were enjoying each other's company.

Shortly after we arrived, I noticed another car pull onto the gravel road and shine a light into the first car that was parked at the entrance. I recognized this as a police light because it was much brighter than the average light. I watched as the officer stopped behind the first car, shined the light but never got out of the vehicle. At this moment, I ran through the mental checklist in my mind. I hadn't noticed a "No Trespassing" sign so I didn't think we were out of line. I knew this wasn't private property because it was a spot that was often frequented by college kids. My friend who recommended this place indicated that it was a popular spot, open to the public. I had my driver's license with me so I didn't think there would be an issue, even though I was driving the car that belonged to my young lady friend. We didn't have any alcohol or other illegal substances with us. So, after quickly running through these things in my mind, I knew we would be alright.

I watched the officer shine the light into the first car and examine the passengers, but he never got out. Then, I saw him slowly move towards us. I expected the same treatment.

The officer drove up slowly and positioned himself directly behind our car and shines the light into the rear window. He shines the light side to side a couple of times. Then, he puts his car in park and exits his police cruiser. He approached my side and after shining the light on me, immediately asked to see my driver's license. While I was getting my license out of my wallet in my back pocket, he shined the light across me and addressed my lady friend, "Ma'am, are you here on your own free will?" She smiled really big and responded, "Yes sir, I am." By this time, I had my license out and handed it to him. He gave it a quick glance, then asked me what we were doing there. I told him that we were watching the planes land and just talking. Without saying a word, he walked around the back of the car and over to the passenger side window. While on the other side of the car, he again shined the light on me, into the back seat, the dash, the floor and then back at my lady friend. He then repeated his question, "Ma'am, are you sure you are here on your own free will?" She again indicated that she was and that we were friends from college. He walked back to my side and handed me my license and then sternly said, "You need to leave!"

He returned to his car and headed down to the third car parked at the end of the lot. As I was driving away, I made a point to notice what he did with the third car. I was looking to see if he got out of his car and asked them to leave as well. He did not. In the rear-view mirror, I noticed his car turn around and then head back towards the exit where we were turning out. After I pulled out, I noticed that he pulled out and turned the same way that I did. He didn't say anything to the two other cars that were there doing the same thing that we were doing.

People of color experience this type of treatment all the time. It's nothing new and, sadly, not unexpected. We have come to expect that white people will be given the benefit of the doubt and that we will not. That is white privilege; the privilege of not having to deal with such blatant preferential treatment based solely on the color of one's skin. White brothers and sisters, we don't fault you for not being aware of this kind of thing happening. How could you, unless you spend time around a person of color like my college friend was doing? However, we are asking that you hear us when we talk about incidents like these that are still happening in America in 2020. Hearing us will help prevent frustrations from building up and boiling over. And, spending more time with people of color wouldn't be a bad idea either. We can learn a lot by spending time with people who don't look or act like we do.

Countless other black and brown people have their own stories like this to tell. When we take the time to listen, we will begin to understand that in America, a difference exists between the way white America views race relations and the way most minorities view it. We have work to do in order for unity to prevail.

In August of 2014, I was the pastor of a church in St. Louis, Missouri. I found myself about five miles away when one of the biggest race confrontations of our generation broke out. Michael Brown, Jr., an 18-year-old African American man, was fatally shot by 28-year-old white police officer, Darren Wilson, in the city of Ferguson, Missouri, a suburb of St. Louis. This event ignited unrest in Ferguson. Before all the facts were reported, protestors believed that Mike Brown was innocently shot by Officer Wilson while his hands were up in the air and he was saying, "Don't shoot." For more than a week, protesters marched through the streets shouting, "Hands up, don't shoot!"

In the midst of this crisis, I found myself in the heart of the city, meeting with people from both sides in an attempt to help keep the peace. Many questions ran through my mind in the days and weeks that followed:

- What should my response be to this and all other highly charged racial conflicts?

- As a black man, what should be my response to the race relations problem in America?
- As a black Christian man, what should my response be?
- As a black Christian man married to a white woman raising five biracial kids, what should my response be?
- As a pastor who has influence over hundreds of men and women of various races and ethnicities, what should my response be?

As I pondered and prayed about this, I remembered the service in 2005 in Denver, when Pastor Bryan Jarrett gave his message. I remembered how the Lord had spoken clearly to Ang and me. God had called us to be a bridge between generations and a bridge between races! It's humbling to see how God has ordained us to be a voice for such a time as this. From before we were even born, He put a plan in place to use us to fulfill His will. We aren't saying that we are the answer to the racial tension in our country, but we are willing to be a part of the solution. We believe that our biracial family makeup, our past ministry experiences, and literally, our DNA, give us credibility and authority to be a voice during this time!

Now we must figure out what to say and when and how to say it. People want to talk about race, racism, race relations. We don't have to look long on social media to see a post that proves this to be true. At times, I use Facebook to offer my point of view. I also talk with friends about race and get their perspectives. Still other times, I get the opportunity to preach about race and explain what I believe to be God's perspective on the subject. God continues to open my eyes to this topic, and show me through His Word how much He has to say about race, racism, and prejudice. As we examine who we are, we must be open to having these conversations.

So, who are we? We are God's children and our Father is in the reconciliation business. He wants to reconcile all men to Him, and He wants us to be reconciled with each other.[3] A few things in this passage of Scripture stand out to me in the Message version. Just like Paul, we are compelled to work urgently with everyone we meet to get them ready to face God.[4] We have to be more concerned about finding ways to work with people. To get along with them. To cooperate. What compels us to do this is Christ's love. As Christians, Christ's love for us and the world compels us in our efforts to reconcile the races.

Racism Today

CHAPTER FOUR

"Racism is still with us. But it is up to us to prepare our children for what they have to meet, and, hopefully, we shall overcome."

– Rosa Parks

4

Racism Today

Racism is real, and it still exists today. Even though our country has made significant progress in advancing the notion that all men are created equal, we still have a long way to go. The sad thing is, this statement itself elicits strong feelings on both sides. Some people agree with me (that we have made advances in race relations throughout the years), while others wholeheartedly disagree. Some claim that the state of our country is no better now than it was in years past. I disagree. Minorities have opportunities for equality and advancement we have not had during any other time in the history of our country. Not only do we have a pathway, but we have laws on our side to protect us from discriminatory practices. In addition, we have the strong support of most of the majority class. I believe most white people are sensitive to the challenges minorities face. Furthermore, I believe that most white people genuinely want to see people of color treated fairly, be afforded the same opportunities they enjoy, and excel in whatever their (our) endeavors. Even though there are still racist people who demonstrate bigotry on a regular basis, our country is not full of racist people. And we must not allow the isolated beliefs and actions of a few to determine how the majority of us think, feel, and act toward one another.

That being said, I want to once again declare that there are still racist people in our country. And it is a big deal, because some of these racist people have power and authority and can make it difficult for minorities to achieve equality. But I believe these people I'm referring to as racists are in the minority, and their racist beliefs and actions are fading away every day. However, two huge factors make it difficult for people to share these beliefs with me.

First, the media is quick to expose any story that hints at racism. Right now, racism is big money business. If there is a news headline that claims racism, people are quick to stop and listen to the story. Racism sells newspapers, magazines, and books, and it brings big ratings to television networks, radio programs, and podcasts. People on both sides of the issue are interested in any story having to do with racism in any way.

I believe the second reason some would disagree with my assessment is because many minorities still experience racism in their everyday experiences. You don't have to look long to find someone who has experienced racism, been called the N-word, been discriminated against, etc. If you have never encountered a person who has "a story," look no further. Allow me to share one of mine.

Like most victims of racism, I can remember the first time. I am sure there were other instances before this, but this is the one that I vividly remember. I asked a white girl to go to prom with me. She accepted my invitation, and we were looking forward to going together. However, just a couple of days before prom, I was asked to meet her at the home of a youth leader from her church. She then informed me she was no longer able to go to prom with me. Her parents objected to her attending prom with a black man. I had known this girl since we were in grade school, and I had no clue her parents felt this way. It was the first time I was ever rejected from anything because of my race. She was upset, embarrassed, and very apologetic. It still hurt. This incident was a clear case of racism. I was being rejected solely because of the color of my skin.

As a person who has not had many instances of racism perpetrated against me (I have had a handful of significant incidents and I'll share more of them later on), I tend to dismiss people who are racist towards me as being ignorant and then move on. I don't let it upset me, and I don't let it change the way I view people of other races. However, victims of racism respond in different ways. Not everyone holds the same view I do.

Many victims of racism get upset and internalize each incident (it is hard not to). In some cases this leads to bitterness and resentment. At times the bitterness and resentment are not only directed towards the perpetrator of the racist act, but toward all people of the perpetrator's race.

Being the victim of racism affects a person on many different levels. There is an emotional, social, intellectual, spiritual, and even physical component to racism.

Emotionally: Racism elicits strong emotions and feelings: hurt, anger, bitterness, rage, shame, inferiority, embarrassment, helplessness, sadness, hate, etc. Depending on what is said or done, and by whom, where, and when – different situations stir up different emotions and feelings. But there is no doubt that racism affects our emotions.

Socially: Because of past experiences, some people won't put themselves in certain social environments. It may cause us to think differently about spending time with certain groups of people. We may want to withdraw or not engage with certain races. All in all, racism changes the way we interact with people.

Intellectually: A person could be secure in their intellectual prowess; nevertheless, when someone makes a racist comment, they are attempting to take a position of power over another person. They are attempting to elevate themselves and put the other person down. It's an attempt to look down on another person. It's natural to have feelings of inferiority when this happens. A natural response is to defend yourself and focus on your credentials to explain why this doesn't apply to you. We want to distance ourselves from the racial stereotypes that paint minorities as unintelligent or intellectually inferior. A person can have a long list of academic letters after their name and still be negatively affected intellectually when hit with a racial epithet. This was a tactic used to keep slaves in line. For centuries, black people were kept from being educated. When we were finally allowed equal access to knowledge, legal loopholes and stumbling blocks were placed in our way, in addition to the racial epithets being used to make us feel inferior.

Spiritually: Those who are harboring bitterness, anger, and resentment because of racist acts are in danger of violating the Holy Scriptures that teach us to forgive. Author and professor of theological and social ethics at Fordham University Bryan N. Massingale said that racism is a sickness of the soul.[5] In a sermon he wrote in 1993, Billy Graham said that racial and ethnic hatred is a sin, and we need to label it as such.[6] Because it is a sin and a sickness of the soul, it affects us spiritually. Both the offender and the victim of racism are affected spiritually. We need God to help us deal with the sin of racism. Christians believe that through Jesus' sacrifice we can get forgiveness and be reconciled to God. So, to find out how we can overcome the sin of racism, we need to look at the example Jesus set. We will go into this more in chapter 9.

Physically: Many aspects of racism effect people physically. First, to become physically shaken up by racist words and actions is not uncommon. I've known people who have been so mad after they were called the N-word that they were physically shaken and unable to focus. Second, other physical effects of racism exist. An article by journalist Sarah Zhang says, "Racism causes stress, and stress can wreak havoc on a person's body and mind. A growing body of research now links experiencing racism to poorer health outcomes—from depression to low-birth weight to cardiovascular disease". [7] Last, an obvious physical effect of racism is seen by all the violence that has been done in the name of racism; obviously, the violence affects people physically. For years racism has led to violent acts which have resulted in people being brutalized and even murdered.

Racism is ugly and hard to deal with. Racism affects us in many different ways, so much so that it's hard to deny the strong emotions and feelings that boil up inside us each time we experience it. When these emotions are stirred up, our initial and most intense response is emotional. While it is important to acknowledge that sometimes our thoughts and feelings are valid, oftentimes they are not. We have to acknowledge that there are times when people make claims of racism that are simply invalid. I'm reminded of an episode of this on the television show, "Blackish." Bow, the female lead and mother on the show, believes an announcer is making racist references at a baseball game about her youngest son, Jack. She calls on her racially-sensitive husband, Dre, to back her up. Dre gets excited to pull out his "race card" and announces that he is always ready to play it. Yet, when he is told what was said and then witnesses what Bow feels is another racist comment, he disagrees with her and puts his race card away, disappointed that he can't play it.[8] This show does a good job of using humor to address some of the racially-sensitive issues of our day. It directly addresses these issues in an over-the-top way, which allows us to use humor while we think about and process the topic at hand.

Richard Pryor also did this in the 70s and 80s. He used humor to address race issues, which got people talking. Dialogue is a good thing.

Today we have a dangerous tendency to label everything as racist. But, labeling stifles conversation. It leaves a person with nowhere else to go. When we keep an open mind and dialogue, we will be able to talk, understand, share, and realize that not everything is racist. Some things have been misperceived and misunderstood. Sometimes people are not aware of offensive or ignorant thoughts and actions. Open dialogue with each other will help us work through some of these things. We must keep in mind that everything isn't racist! I want to introduce a few terms I've been using lately to help make the distinctions I'm referencing.

1) Racism is not a new term. It's having the idea that one's own race is superior and has the right to dominate others. Racists believe other racial groups are inferior to their race.

I can remember a few times in my life being called the N-word, which is a blatant example of racism. Once, in college, I was with a handful of teammates from my football team. It was late at night, and we were all hungry, so I borrowed my parents' minivan, and we all went to get food. We were pulling out of the drive-through lane, and another car was in the drive lane attempting to exit at the same time. It was unclear as to who had the right of way, but I proceeded towards the exit, thinking it was me. My friend A. Ray was in the passenger seat and noticed that the other driver approached us quickly, as if he wasn't going to stop. A. Ray gave him a look, and the driver yelled back at him, "Get out of the way, you stupid n!&*$!" Big mistake! This unknowing white dude wasn't aware that we had a van full of big football players, most of us black, but all of us ready to throw down! When he saw us all coming his way, he was quick to repeatedly apologize and back down, saying he didn't want any trouble. Wisdom prevailed that day, because although we were all heated and ready to lay the smack down, we returned to our car and went back to school.

I don't know why some people are quick to throw the N-word out there. It's an automatic invitation to a physical altercation. This particular guy didn't count the cost of his actions before letting that derogatory insult fly. Most racists don't. That's why, after the fact, and once the consequences of such hate speech come upon them, they go on their apology tours.

2) Racial Ignorance includes being unaware of possibly-offensive words or actions. This involves being uninformed of racially-sensitive things, but not having ill intent or motives to elevate one race over the other.

Growing up in my small rural town of Macomb, Illinois, I was not exposed to a lot of Latino people. I pretty much remember people either being black or white. This was the case all throughout college and up until I moved to Ft. Myers, Florida. There were noticeably more diverse people groups in Ft. Myers than I had ever been around before.

I was a part of a large church that celebrated diversity and offered church services that catered to different ethnicities. From the adults down to the youth, the church was diverse. As part of my job responsibilities, I gave oversight to the youth pastors on our other campuses. I remember a time that I accompanied our Spanish youth group on a trip. It was the first time I had ever been around so many Latino people. We had a good time, joking, laughing, and getting to know each other. On the way home, we ended up stopping at a McDonald's for dinner. About sixty students were in the front lobby ordering food. I noticed that although they all were Latino, they had very different physical traits and characteristics. As I was standing at the back of the line waiting to order food, I asked the youth pastor if all of the students were Mexican. Now, mind you, this question was posed to the youth pastor, in the middle of a conversation between her and me only, right there in the middle of a loud and busy lobby with 60 students trying to order food. I don't know how they all heard me, but they all did! All other interactions stopped for that brief moment. Everyone paused their conversation, turned and stared at me, looked me up and down, and then proceeded to directly address me, setting the record straight about where they were from... **"No, I'm not Mexican!"** most all of them exclaimed! Then they proudly proceeded to inform me about where they were from, all in unison.

> "I'm from Puerto Rico. . ."
> "I'm from Columbia. . ."
> "I'm from the Domincan Republic. . ."
> "I'm from Brazil. . ."
> "I'm from Venezuela. . ."
> "I'm from Ecuador. . ."
> "I'm from Bolivia. . ."

"I'm from Guatemala. . ."
"I'm from Chile. . ."

I just didn't know. I had never been around many Latino people at this point in my life. I was extremely ignorant. I wasn't even educated as to all the different countries they could have been from. This is a prime example of racial ignorance. I was quick to take ownership of this misstep by throwing my hands up and saying, "My bad, my bad," over and over. I'm thankful for the graciousness of all the students who gave me a pass on this one. We laughed it off and went on with the rest of the trip and had a great time.

3) Racial Insensitivity is when we knowingly or unknowingly fail to consider how our actions could be perceived as offensive to other races.

Several years ago, while attending a wedding in my hometown of Fort Pierce, Florida, I had an encounter that many others would not have easily dismissed. One of my cousins was getting married, and both my wife and I were in the wedding. I sang a song during the ceremony, and my wife was one of the bridesmaids.

Ang was pregnant at the time, and needed to have an alteration made to her dress after the ceremony so she could use it again if she had occasion. *Side note*: I don't know why she ever thought she would use a silky forest green bridesmaid dress ever again in her life, because she never did.

Anyway, after the wedding, we went to the house of the tailor who had made the bridesmaids' dresses. She was a little, old, white Floridian who was well into her 80s. She also happened to be a friend of my cousin, the bride. She was nice and friendly and extremely talkative. She made it known that she was a lifelong Florida Gators fan and wouldn't have any other colors represented in her house. It turned out that she had been at the wedding and heard me sing. She wanted to compliment me on the beautiful song. She said; "Are you that Negro boy who sang that beautiful song? I really can't tell because all of you look alike." What? I mean, I know she was in her 80s, and the words "negro" and "boy" were probably a step up from what she was used to calling us in her day, but come on! How insensitive could she be?

Part of the reason we have such a big divide in our country is because one side wants us to think that everything is racist. That perspective will keep us preoccupied with fighting against each other. We will be distracted and unable to work together to resolve real problems like homelessness, drug addiction, gun violence, urban decay, poverty, babies being born out of wedlock, and, most importantly, sharing the love of Christ with those who have not yet experienced it for themselves.

Some people want us to think we are living in a post-racist society, with the proof being that we elected our first black President, Barack Obama. They say we are much better than we were years ago. They say the dream that MLK had has been realized. This is partially true. Things are better than they used to be. MLK's dream is being realized – but we have not arrived yet. Minorities do have the opportunity to pursue the American dream, but we must be honest about the fact that there is still more work to be done!

While we are working to achieve the dream, we must differentiate between racism, racial ignorance, and racial insensitivity. This will allow people space to interact, dialogue, and work together without fear of messing up and being labeled a racist. Discussion ends once a label is assigned. Neither the labeler nor the one labeled sees any reason to continue to discuss the race issue at that point. I would suggest that in our society today, being labeled a racist is one of the worst labels you can be given. Once that description is placed on you, it feels as if there is nothing else you can do or say. Everything you say can and will be used against you. You carry that stigma for life. No one can cosign for you to bring you back into good graces with the masses. This is the danger in thinking that everything is racist. Everything is NOT racism! Some things may be racially ignorant or racially insensitive but not racist.

Governor Matt Bevin from Kentucky said, "So many are quick to decry any comments they don't agree with to be racist. If everything is racist we diminish the reality that racism truly exists."[9] This is so true. We have to allow room for people to share opposing thoughts and views about sensitive subjects, including race, without fear of being labeled a racist.

I think for something to be labeled "racist," there needs to be actual intent to be racist. But the truth is we don't always know everyone's intent. So, why not give the benefit of the doubt and dialogue with people when there are perceived instances of racism versus assuming their motives and intentions?

I had an incident in a department store in the mall in Springfield Missouri, a few months ago. The clerk was a nice white lady who was very talkative. During the course of our conversation, she found out that we lived in Kansas City, and she informed us that she used to live near our suburb. She explained that she used to work for this department store when she lived there as well. She went on to tell us about the closing of the store. But before she did, she paused and gave her disclaimer. I knew what was coming; I've experienced this a few times in the past. She said, "Now I'm not racist, but our store in the mall closed down because the black people came in and ran down the store."

She went on to say that she has nothing against black people, but implied that a lot of issues were brought into that store and the whole mall because black people moved into the neighborhood. And to further prove she was not a racist, she went on to tell us about the black members of her family.

I believe this lady was racially insensitive and even racially ignorant. Even though I imagine that many people will disagree with me, I don't think she was being racist. She was open and honest enough to have a dialogue with me and Ang, a black man and his white wife, most likely because she felt safe enough to express it. I don't agree with her assessment of why the mall was closed, but I realize that her experience caused her to believe the way she did. It would have been easy for me to label her a racist and dismiss her or berate her. But I chose not to do either of those things. I walked away from a conversation with no ill feelings toward her (or people of her race) because I believe she was being racially insensitive and was, in fact, racially ignorant. Those things are easier to forgive. I didn't feel animosity toward her because I did not perceive her intentions to be racist. Had I perceived her to be racist, however, animosity would have popped right into my heart. For example, what if she had refused to conduct our sale or asked us to leave the store because she feared that yet another store would be closed due to "black people running the place down?" Racism is a lot harder to forgive. And, unfortunately, and to our nation's detriment, many people refuse to do so.

I cannot say this enough: I believe that racism still exists. And, for the record, it is extremely offensive when white people try to deny or downplay that fact. Just because you may not see it or experience it doesn't mean it's not happening all around you. If you don't think racism still exists, I have to ask the question, "Are you engaging with anyone outside of your race?" I can't help but think that the only way you wouldn't notice it is if you aren't around other races. It doesn't take long to see racism when two people of different races encounter each other in the world today. 'Starting again' is going to take us realizing that although we have come a long way in improving race relations, we still have a lot of work left to do. This doesn't invalidate the progress. It just means we need to keep working to achieve unity. Unity through conversation. Unity through engagement. Unity through relationships. Unity through prayer.

Whose Side Am I On?

CHAPTER FIVE

"Now is the time to make justice a reality for all of God's children."
– Martin Luther King, Jr.

5

Whose Side Am I On?

For as long as human beings have been around, people have been leery of those who are different from them. Human nature tends to distrust the unfamiliar. This seems reasonable when it comes to experiences, things like trying new foods, going to new places, and doing new things. However, when this same level of guardedness is shown toward people, things can get ugly. Leeriness easily devolves into dislike. Different becomes threatening.

The color of one's skin often stands out as the biggest difference between people. Their skin is different from mine; therefore, they are different from me. I am leery of those who are different from me. I feel threatened by people who are different from me.

Once people feel threatened, their attitudes and actions change to reflect that perceived threat. Because familiarity is comforting, we attempt to protect ourselves by surrounding ourselves with it and by building up barriers between us (the familiar, the same as) and them (the unfamiliar, the different). And, because familiar makes us feel safe and good, we easily draw the conclusion that people who are like me are better than the people who are not. Racism is born. People begin to discriminate against people of other races because they think their own race is superior. One side is good, and the other side must somehow, inevitably, be bad.

The frequency with which this happens in society has led some to believe that racism is part of human nature.[10] It is commonly assumed that racism is as old as human society itself. Racism is found all around the world. America just happens to have a more recent and horrific past when it comes to racism.

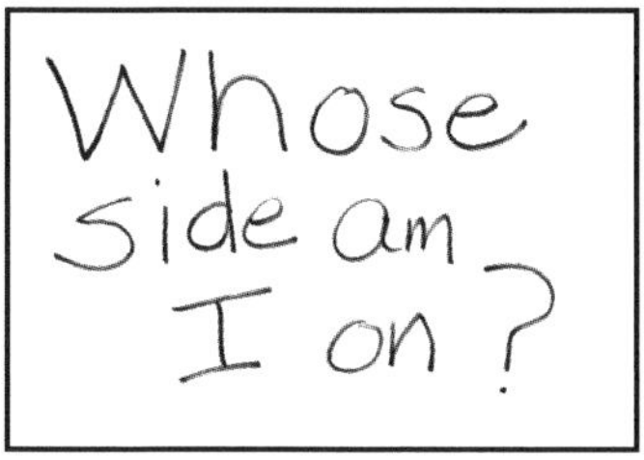

Much animosity exists in the black community over racism, discrimination, and slavery. And no wonder, considering it has been well documented that for centuries in America, black slaves were treated like animals.[11] Furthermore, people commonly believe our country was founded on racism. It's hard to disagree with the notion that America has a history of oppressing people of color.

White people living in the twenty- first century are often confused as to why there is animosity over the racism that took place in our nation's past. They are not as likely as individuals of color to feel the effects of racism in their day-to-day lives, so they don't see the connection between our country's past racial sins and the current racial divide.

Our past haunts us so much that people of all colors live in fear of being labeled as racist. I create social media posts from time to time that get people thinking and talking about race issues. These posts usually generate a good deal of public conversation, but I inevitably receive several private messages from people unwilling to express their opinions publicly for fear of being labeled racist.

The rise of political correctness and racial sensitivity has everyone on high alert. It seems like the battle lines have been drawn, and everyone is asking us to pick a side. If you fail to choose a side, don't worry, a side will be chosen for you. Based on your beliefs, affiliations, and voiced opinions, you will be labeled—conservative or liberal, right or left, Republican or Democrat. There is no middle ground anymore, no room for compromise, and no trying to remain neutral. Whose side are you on? That's the question. Here are your choices:

- The people vs. the police
- Republican vs. Democrat
- Black nationalist vs. white supremacist
- Us vs. them

It's hard to even see middle ground, let alone find people willing to meet there. This isn't new; it's been this way for generations. Black people and white people are terribly unfamiliar with each other's perspectives. As we have already established, mankind feels threatened by the unfamiliar, by things we don't understand. A natural defense is to pull others around us who are like us, who are familiar to us. Black people and white people have gone to their separate corners, ready to fight when the time comes. So, the question remains, whose side are you on?

Are we on the side of the police or the people?

As I have indicated, the issue in Dallas was the impetus for me to make our viral video. The country is divided, and it seems the divide is growing larger each day between those who support the police and those who don't. Police officers feel undervalued, underappreciated, and disrespected. They don't feel they have the support of the people they took an oath to serve and protect, nor of the government officials to whom they report. This past week, I saw a news report that showed police officers in New York City being violated as they responded to a call in the line of duty. People were jeering them and letting it be known they were not welcome in their communities. People actually had the nerve, in broad daylight, to throw buckets of water on the police officers as they were simply trying to do their job. That level of immaturity and disrespect is ridiculous and very disappointing.

This issue of the people versus the police stems from recent incidents which involve black people being shot by police officers. We can argue over whether or not to label it an epidemic, but we can't argue over the fact that these incidents have forever changed our country. Cameras on cell phones have captured many incidents of police brutality and of police officers killing unarmed black men. The media has made sure to cover these events nonstop. Politicians have made this issue central to their election campaigns. Our country is divided. We are all being asked to make a choice of which side we want to be on. However, we can reject the demand to pick a side and make that choice. What if we want to be on the side of the police *and* the people?

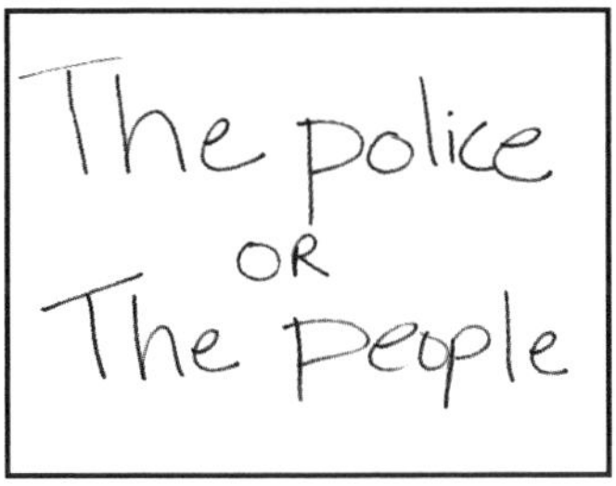

With this in mind, we've decided not to make this discussion about choosing a side. Our goal is to bring unity into every situation. Therefore, we believe we can support *both* the people *and* the police.

In order to do so, we understand it will be necessary to address the issues contributing to the division: things like policing in urban neighborhoods, traffic light cameras, and police brutality, as well as the defiance and disrespect that many police officers are now being subjected to. We are not saying that we have all the answers, but we would like to begin a discussion. It's time to bring both sides together and bring solutions to the table.

Are we on the side of black people or white people?

In the darkness, we are faced with this question that is meant to divide us! This false choice is straight from the Devil. Such a divisive question shouldn't surprise us, since it comes from our enemy, whose purpose is to kill, steal, and destroy.[12] His strategy is to divide and conquer. I fear that too many Christian people are playing right into his hand. We fail to realize he is using one of his oldest strategies in the book – racism – to keep us distracted and fighting with each other, blinded by hatred or fear of the unknown. We are like defenseless sheep moving around mindlessly, while the wolf is planning his attack. We have failed to realize this race issue is a spiritual issue.

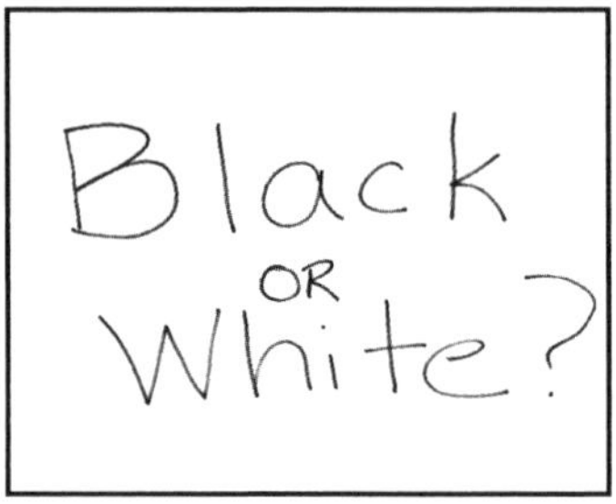

Think about it; before there was black versus white hatred, there was Jew versus Gentile racism. Racism divided people and cultures as soon as the world was big enough to be diverse.

And, unfortunately, racism perpetuates itself. For example, even though Jews were looked down on by the Romans, they thought they were better than Samaritans. They wanted nothing to do with them.[13] Jews in biblical times would often travel from Galilee to Judea. The Jews despised Samaritans so much that they didn't even want to walk through Samaria. One main road led from Jerusalem past Bethany to Jericho, then north up the Jordan Valley and the west side of the Sea of Galilee to Capernaum. A second, more direct route to Judea would take the Jews directly through Samaria. To avoid Samaria, whose inhabitants the Jews despised, Jews often traveled the longer, less direct road when traveling between Galilee and Judea.[14]

Similarly, today, we see blacks and whites going out of their way to avoid interacting with each other. This is not the way God intended His children to act. Jesus addressed this issue in the Parable of the Good Samaritan. He didn't want His disciples to look at the color of skin or nationality—essentially, to be racist—but, rather, to aspire to a higher standard of simply loving everyone.[15]

Do I have to pick a side?

I propose that we reject the false narrative of choosing a side. As a Christian, my allegiance is to the kingdom of God. God's mission and God's purpose are my number one priority.

If I'm not careful, I can forget this very easily. That is why I consistently spend time reading the Bible. I want to always stay connected to God and to hear Him speak to me through His Word.

The Bible says, "my sheep will know my voice."[16] By staying close to God, and by listening to His voice, I am certain that I won't be confused about whose side I should be on. I'm on His side. And He is on the side of all who belong to Him, regardless of skin color.

Scripture teaches us that the Lord is with us when we are with Him. When we seek Him, we will find Him.[17] It's our job to make sure we are with Him. Perhaps we need to spend more time seeking God's perspective on the issues of the day. It never works out well to try and do things our own way and then expect God to come in later and bless our mess. You would be wise to make sure you are always staying close to God so that He will stay close to you.

God doesn't pick a side. He loves people on every side. He loves all people so much that He sent His Son to die for all people, no matter the race. We will go into this more in Chapter 7.

Dr. Martin Luther King, Jr. dreamt of a day when all races would unite, not pick a side. Just as Dr. King and his contemporaries led the nation in racial reconciliation, we believe that the Church should reposition itself to lead the racial reconciliation in this generation. We are the ones who should facilitate dialogue. We have access to the One who gave His life to reconcile God and mankind. We can show the world what reconciliation looks like. Remember, our allegiance is to the Kingdom of God. He wants to bring peace and unity to all people. We do not have to pick a side.

Unfortunately, the Church is not leading, and others have risen up to attempt to lead the race conversation in America. However, attempting to solve the race problem without the power of the One who is The Way, The Truth, and The Life will not bring about love, forgiveness, unity, or peace. Rather than proclaiming the light of God's love over the racial divide, these leaders offer messages of payback, restitution, and guilt. It is as if they are proposing that in order to correct the wrongs of racism, white people should switch places with black people. Some people would like to see the pendulum swing all the way to the other side so that white people can see what it feels like to be on the bottom. This is ridiculous (not to mention impossible). Instead, I propose that both sides unite and begin to combat the powers of darkness trying to divide us. We don't have to pick a side. In fact, we must *not* pick a side!

CHAPTER SIX

Mistakes

"Being teachable means you are willing to learn things that you thought you already knew."
– Coach Tom Mullins

6

Mistakes

Both sides have made mistakes:

In his book *The Seven Habits of Highly Effective People*, Stephen Covey encourages his readers to "Seek first to understand, then to be understood."[18] Covey presents this habit as the most important principle of interpersonal relations. He's challenging us to learn how to communicate clearly, and that starts with listening to others. Effective listening is not simply echoing what the other person has said through the lens of one's own experience. Rather, it is putting oneself in the perspective of the other person, listening empathically for both feeling and meaning.[19] Let's keep this in mind as we tackle the issue of how both sides have made mistakes. The goal is to seek to fully understand what the other side is saying. Until we commit to listening, to the point of understanding, we will not have true progress in race relations. The lack of understanding causes people to retreat further into their corners in an effort to regroup and prepare for the next round of the fight.

Let's start with the big one: slavery. Slavery was inarguably the greatest offense committed against black people in our nation's history. Even though it was abolished over 150 years ago, the repercussions still impact our world. One particular area of pain that still resonates with many black Americans is that the Bible was often used to defend the practices of slavery, segregation, and prejudice. For example, many Christian slave owners believed the Bible provided all the justification they needed to enslave their fellowman.[20] It is offensive to black people that God's Word was used to justify this great evil. Some black people can't accept that the Holy Scriptures once used in such a way could now be relevant to them in any way.

In fairness, when speaking of America's racist history, it should be noted that not all of the American forefathers wanted slavery to continue. Thomas Jefferson and the majority of the forefathers were growing weary of slavery at the time of the fight for colonial independence. Jefferson blamed King George III for bringing slavery to America. By the time of the Revolutionary War, only two states allowed the importation of slaves. Trading and owning slaves was still allowed in all the states, but the tide was changing in America.[21] A simple look back demonstrates the volatile history America has had with racism, prejudice, and slavery.

After slavery was abolished, the people in power continued to subjugate black people through tenant farming and sharecropping. Sharecropping became widespread in the South as a response to economic upheaval caused by the end of slavery. The message sent to black people was, "Even though you aren't slaves anymore, you still can't own property nor strive to achieve the American dream!"

This was the unofficial beginning of institutional racism, although it wasn't officially labeled as such for decades. Institutional racism (also known as systemic racism) is a form of racism expressed in the practice of social and political institutions. It is reflected in disparities regarding wealth, income, criminal justice, employment, housing, health care, political power, and education, among other factors.[22] Basically, the people in power set up systems to keep their power. Institutional racism effects many aspects of black and brown people's lives; where they live, the quality of the education they receive, their income, types of food they have access to, whether they have access to clean air, clean water or adequate medical treatment, and the types of interactions they have with the criminal justice system. The roots of institutional racism are often hidden in social, economic, and political systems.[23] For years, white people in power developed and maintained institutional racism to keep black people in their place. Jim Crow Laws, enacted in the late 1800s and enforced until 1965, were used to exponentially widen the divide between the races. The damaging results of these laws and the separate but equal mentality are still being experienced in America today. For example, it's common knowledge that we have "black" churches and "white" churches in communities of all sizes.

Segregation was the law of the land for many years and was used by white people to limit the freedom of brown and black people. Then, in an effort to end race-based segregation within American public and private schools, the courts ordered school integration and desegregation busing. This was an attempt towards racial reconciliation, but many white people rejected this. When black and brown people moved into their schools, communities, and neighborhoods, many white people moved out. This is a practice known as white flight (which is defined as the phenomenon of white people moving out of urban areas, particularly those with significant minority populations, and into suburban areas).[24] When the white people moved out, they took the factories, businesses, and jobs with them which lead to urban decay. Urban decay is the sociological process by which a previously functioning city, or part of a city, falls into disrepair and decrepitude.[25] All of these wrongs are now officially recorded in history as mistakes propagated by white people.

These grievous mistakes from the past have established a framework in which black people have many hurdles to cross before they get to a level playing field with white contemporaries. Things like racial profiling, institutional racism, and urban decay are not struggles many white people face. The past mistakes of the white community have been identified by all people and acknowledged by most people. We do not need to exacerbate these past wrongs by continuing to assign blame and demanding retribution. No one alive today owned slaves. Therefore, no one is guilty of the sin of slavery. No one owes penance. However, I, like many of my other black brothers and sisters, want our white brothers and sisters to be sensitive to the negative effects that the institution of slavery and other racist institutions still have on our society. Please do not ignore or deny the fact that it's still more difficult to be a person of color in America than it is to be a white person. We call that white privilege (another controversial subject we will address later).

The people versus the police

As I'm writing this chapter, the news is reporting that a New York City judge has ruled that police officer Daniel Pantaleo should be fired following his controversial involvement in the death of Eric Garner. For me, this is a clear case of unnecessary police brutality. But for others, it's not so clear. I've listened to those who support the police officer, and they say that Eric Garner disobeyed a lawful command and was resisting arrest. This is true. However, others would say, and many agree, that this was definitely a case of excessive force. Eric Garner should still be alive today, and yet, he's not. I'll admit, I don't understand the mindset that it's ever acceptable to resist arrest or to disobey a command from a police officer. I have been taught to obey in the moment and to fight it out in court later, if necessary. This takes a great deal of self-restraint, especially when it feels as though an officer is wrong or abusing his or her authority, but I think it makes more sense than to resist arrest and escalate the situation and risk becoming the next sensational news story.

I have friends and family members who are police officers, and they tell me that every time they make an arrest, they are on high alert. Each and every time, they are concerned for their own safety because, "you never know what the assailant will do." They have families who are fearful for their safety and want to see them make it home at the end of their shift. I can understand why a police officer would want their lawful commands to be obeyed.

With that being said, this case doesn't pass the common sense test. There was no need for the excessive force that led to a man being choked to death, on the street, in broad daylight, after saying that he couldn't breathe eleven times. Eric Garner literally couldn't breathe. Many other black men and women are figuratively saying "we can't breathe," because of the excessive force and unfair policing practices that are often witnessed by people of color in our communities.

Recent cell phone videos have documented incidents which clearly show that, more times than they care to admit, police have been in the wrong. This has been a problem for years (an issue rooted in the imbalance of power associated with slavery and the Jim Crow era mentioned above). But, like I said, thanks to video and social media, we are getting more and more undeniable evidence of the issue. Some people are true victims of police brutality, but not everyone.

On the other hand, it seems that some people of color are not willing to admit the mistakes we have made in our interactions with the police. As I previously stated, I lived in St. Louis during the Ferguson/Mike Brown incident. I was on the streets of Ferguson during the protesting. I saw the emotions of people leading up to violent clashes. I heard firsthand the personal stories of police wrongdoing, excessive use of force, and police brutality from the people on the streets of Ferguson. I witnessed the tension felt by people on both sides. I spoke to police officers who were on the front line trying to keep the peace. It was very intense.

Once I examined the evidence, I realized we had been fed a false narrative. I wish Mike Brown hadn't been killed, but the evidence is overwhelming that he was in the wrong by charging the cop and trying to get the officer's gun. Even the Department of Justice (under black Attorney General Eric Holder) concluded this. And yet, there was still looting, rioting, and violent protesting. With my own eyes, I saw businesses burned down, many of which were never reopened. I personally spoke to minority business owners who had worked hard to serve the people in their own community, yet had their shops destroyed. Many of these small business owners didn't have insurance and stood to lose everything they had worked so hard to build.

We have to admit that the black community was in the wrong regarding the destructive response to this perceived injustice all based on a false narrative. If I were to say no more, this is proof of the point I made about both sides being wrong. And yet, some may disagree and say that rioting and peaceful protests (although some protesting has not been peaceful) are not wrong. To that I will simply add this disclaimer: The impetus for making our video was the police officers being shot in Dallas. I believe that just because we have been wronged (and we have been), doesn't mean anyone should kill police officers! There is no justification for the deaths of the fallen officers. This is what I had in mind when I said that both sides have made mistakes.

A second way in which the black community has made mistakes is evidenced by the high number of black people committing crimes, which only heightens the racial profiling problem we face.

> Both sides have made mistakes

Obviously, not all black people are in the wrong, but black people have indeed made mistakes that have contributed to the problem we face today. This is something we need to address in our communities.

My last point concerning the mistakes black people have made concerns the disrespect and loathing of police officers. It's never justifiable to protest by calling for police officers to be killed. This happened at a Black Lives Matter rally in New York City when protesters were heard shouting, "What do we want? Dead pigs in a blanket."[26] There is no place for this type of rhetoric in our society. This disrespect of the police is being taught to our kids in minority communities. Obviously, the police have made mistakes. And, thankfully, videos have exposed the mistreatment that many blacks and other minorities have been experiencing for years. But, none of us are better off in our communities when we teach distrust and disrespect of police officers who are here to serve and protect. By and large, the majority of police officers are good people who are committed to serving and protecting all people, no matter their race.

Some folks look to these issues and are quick to point out that, until black communities clean up their act (so to speak), they don't have a right to express their concerns about police brutality. That is nonsense and definitely not the point I am making. We can and should work on these problems simultaneously. At the same time we are seeking equal justice in terms of racial profiling and police brutality, we need to be seeking equal justice for victims of crime and violence brought on by people in our own community.

If you still aren't convinced both sides have made mistakes, please remember that when I put this statement in the video, it was just days after a horrible mistake one of our own made: the attack on the Dallas police officers as retaliation for previous incidents of police brutality. I stand by my belief that it's never acceptable to target and kill police officers who have taken a pledge to serve and protect us all.

I do not apologize for my controversial statement, nor do I believe I was off in my assessment. Here's why: I do my best to incorporate Covey's 5th Habit in my everyday life. I try to seek to understand other people's perspectives before I try to convince them of my points of view. I strive to interact and dialogue with a diverse group of people in an effort to understand what they are saying. As well, I constantly interact on social media and in person with people who are willing to share their views on cultural and social issues. I want to know their perspectives. When you take time to listen to people, they will tell you what you have done to offend them. Since I have taken the time to hear from both black and white people, to understand why they are offended, it has become clear to me that both sides have indeed made mistakes.

We have to be willing to open our eyes and be truthful if we want reconciliation, unity, and peace. This is what our message is all about! Let's come together and solve these problems rather than create a bigger divide by holding onto the us versus them mindset.

Both sides share the blame

When we acknowledge that both sides have made mistakes, it leads us to the realization that both sides share the blame. In the wake of all that is happening to black and brown people in our culture – racism being experienced from coast to coast, unarmed black men being shot by police, and a heightened awareness of past discriminatory practices and policies – it's difficult for some to put any blame on the minority community. Although this is a hard statement for us to acknowledge, it is true that both sides share the blame. Both sides are guilty of misunderstanding the other side. Both sides have been guarded and hesitant to come together. Both sides have failed to bring about racial unity. And both sides share the blame. We must be willing to acknowledge this truth in order to 'start again'.

We don't hold this point of view so we can hold one race liable. We are not assigning blame. We are not calling for reparations or resolution statements. However, in order for us to move forward in love, forgiveness, unity, and peace, both sides have to acknowledge our mistakes so we can begin to build trust.

I've spoken with white people who say, "We have admitted past wrongs done by the white community, and we want to make things right. Yet, it seems like some black people are not willing to admit their wrongs." They offer a few examples. White people tell me stories of how they have worked with black people who, without cause, were untrusting of them and defensive, from the time they first met them. They tell me stories of encountering black people who have a chip on their shoulder. They are hostile toward white people and often make rude or cynical comments. Other white people express to me that some black people appear to be racist themselves, and are purposefully offensive because they hold the view that black people can't be racist.

I've heard from white people who point out that the black community as a whole isn't willing to admit past mistakes. They say black people usually side with other black people, even when one of their own is guilty or in the wrong. They use the O.J. Simpson trial and the Bill Cosby case as examples. It seems as though it's difficult for black people to assign guilt to one of our own, even when the evidence overwhelmingly points to guilt. I'm ready to admit that it took me over 20 years to finally admit that I think O.J. did it. Another white person brought up a recent example of this with the Jussie Smollett hate crime case. Smollett told police that he was attacked outside his apartment building by two men in ski masks who called him racial and homophobic slurs and said "This is MAGA country," referencing President Donald Trump's slogan "Make America Great Again."[27]

Others point out that if a white person makes a negative comment about President Obama, there is a good chance they will be accused of doing this because they are racist. They aren't believed when they say they are expressing their dislike of his policies, not him personally, and that their opinion has nothing to do with race. Many white people say that when they criticize President Obama, black people as a whole attack them. Their belief is that we can sometimes be blinded by the color of our skin. Black people, we need to ask ourselves if there is any truth to this.

Let me be clear, I'm not saying that black people share the blame for racism. I'm referring to racial reconciliation and the prolongation of hate, division, and disunity. There is enough blame to be shared by all for the hesitancy to come together in racial unity.

So, who is ultimately to blame for racism? Shall we blame God? No! God doesn't like one race of people more than He likes another. If that were the case, God could be considered to be racist. Obviously, He is not. In fact, since racism is a sin, God does not like racism. The Bible teaches us that God does not take delight in wickedness.[28] Therefore, it would be silly for us to blame Him for racism. Humans are to blame for racism. People choose, through their own free will,[29] whether they will be racist or not. We are challenging people to choose not to be racist. We strongly believe that with God's help, all human beings have the ability to avoid the sin of racism. Fourth century British theologian Pelagius argued that God has endowed human beings with certain abilities—for example, the ability to avoid sin.[30] God gave humans the gift of free will. We all need to choose whether we will exercise our free will to do good or to do evil. When we choose to do good, we are choosing to be on God's side.

Both sides share the blame

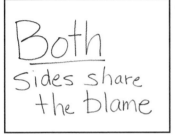

Therefore, God cannot be blamed for racism, just like He cannot be blamed for murder, or lying, or stealing. Racism can be blamed on people who abuse power, but not on God. He is not a racist.

Let's talk about the "N-word"

The use of the N-word word has caused both sides to make mistakes. Throughout American history, white people have used this word to demean black people. And yet, somewhere along the line, black people chose to use this word with each other and embrace it. Today, the word is used by both sides in various contexts to express either love or hate. That's very confusing! Both sides are still messing this one up! The word continues to be used, even though we believe it is highly distasteful, and most would agree there is no place for it to be used in our society anymore.

Obviously, it's always a mistake for white people to use this word. It's offensive to hear a white person use it. A look at our illicit American history reveals that there is no good way that a white person can use the N-word. Black people were demeaned with that word for so many years by white people that it cannot be redeemed. But what about black people? Is there a place for it to be used in black culture?

I did an informal poll of about 25 of my black friends and relatives, and I was surprised by their response. Most of them believe there is absolutely no place for the N-word to be used today (in any setting). One of my friends said she didn't grow up using that word and she still doesn't use it now. She doesn't want anyone of any color feeling comfortable calling her the N-word. She's a young professional and holds the strong belief that there is no room in society for such a divisive word. Many agree with her. I would say the common belief now, among both black and white people, is that no one should use the N-word.

But there are many black people who still use the N-word and think it's acceptable for them to do so. The belief that no one should use the word, not even black people, is difficult for them to accept. I'll admit, I struggle with this as well. Like many others, I grew up using the N-word around my black friends and family. It wasn't until a couple of years ago that I discontinued this practice. Some black people still believe they have the freedom to use it in certain settings and view this as somewhat of a birthright. They don't want anyone, including the political correctness police, telling them they can't use the word anymore. Their view is that as long as they use the word responsibly, they are good.

They follow the unofficial rules for using the N-word:

- Only use it around other black people.
- Never put the "er" at the end. The proper ending is with an "a."
- Never use it in a professional environment, only in personal settings.
- Never use it around white people! Unless . . .
  - Said white person is a close friend who understands black culture.
  - Said white person is a white girl who has shown to be "down with dating brothas."
  - Puerto Ricans and Mexicans can use it if they are close friends.

It seems that most black people have heard of these rules and do their best to abide by them – except for . . . black rappers, artists, comedians, and singers. They are the worst at dropping the N-word, especially in their music. Many black rappers, singers, and recording artists won't seem to let that word rest. Ironically, they are the first ones to get upset when a white person uses it. I was shocked by the story of a white woman being booed at a Kendrick Lamar concert after he invited her on stage to sing. She was singing the song the way he wrote it and didn't leave out the N-word, so he stopped her, and the crowd booed her. [31]

Should we blame white music executives and producers for creating a culture in the hip hop industry that perpetuates using the N-word? One of my friends said; "Umm, a little. But I think this is shifting the personal responsibility from us to them. That is a victim mentality. We don't have to listen to music filled with N-this and N-that. We certainly don't have to buy it." My friend is right.

Furthermore, there are enough black producers, executives, and label owners that we could start changing this culture if we really wanted to. Jay-Z,[32] Kanye,[33] P. Diddy,[34] Dr. Dre,[35] Snoop Dogg,[36] Russell Simmons,[37] Tech N9ne,[38] and Master P[39] — these are all black men who have founded and/or own music labels. They are in charge of the content that is produced by themselves and their artists. They have been for decades. They could produce music void of the N-word. They have had enough time to positively change the culture, if they truly wanted to. Yet they are at the forefront of objectifying our people by continuing to produce music littered with the N-word.

As for the artists themselves, there are many black artists who can say whatever they want and still have their music remain at the top of the charts. No one is telling Beyoncé or Nikki Minaj what they can or can't say. Tech N9ne writes, produces, and sells whatever he wants. Jay-Z[32] and Kanye[33] can put anything out there, and people will buy it. And who do you think buys their music? Mostly white adult males.[40] White people are hearing our black musicians and entertainers continue to use the N-word and feel comfortable enough to repeat what they are hearing. Whose fault is this? Black people, we have to own our part in this and stop blaming white people for everything that holds us back.

The truth is, both sides share the blame for the continued use of such a derogatory word. The good news is, both sides can be a part of the solution. I believe our society is ready to put this divisive word to death, once and for all. This is just the beginning.

When we choose to 'start again', we will endeavor to choose our words more carefully. Let's choose positive and uplifting words instead of divisive and derogatory language. The Bible says that the words of the reckless pierce like swords, but the tongue of the wise brings healing.[41] Sometimes the words people use are very cutting to the person at whom they are directed.

Christians need to remember that the Bible teaches us that we wrestle not against flesh and blood but against Satan and his evil forces.[42] When we realize this, we understand that none of us are ultimately to blame. Satan is the guilty one. He's the one who has used racism, segregation, prejudice, and slavery to hinder the spread of the Gospel by trying to force us to pick a side. As we endeavor to bring light to this world, we will demonstrate we are on God's side, and no other side matters.

CHAPTER SEVEN

We Are in this Together

"Let us not seek the Republican answer or the Democratic answer, but the right answer. Let us not seek to fix the blame for the past. Let us accept our own responsibility for the future."

– John F. Kennedy

7

We are in this Together

We are all humans

We may be different colors, shapes, sizes, and ethnicities, but we are all still part of the human race. In the emails we have received, many people have commented that, although we may be different on the outside, we all bleed the same. How much better would our country be if the first thing we noticed about each person was his or her heart, personality, or character. These are what truly define people. Hopefully those are the things that we choose to focus on and remember. I believe it is basically dishonest to pretend we don't see physical characteristics. Things like hair color, size, height, and, yes, even skin color—it's normal and acceptable for us to notice these things about people and to use them to describe each other.

When people meet me, they will quickly observe three noticeable physical characteristics I possess. I call them the three Bs. I am a *big, bald, black* man! These are accurate words. I don't mind that people use them to describe me. In fact, I use them to describe myself. I don't mind if they recognize me as a big, bald, black man, because that is an accurate description of me. However, that description doesn't define me. It doesn't tell anyone anything else about me other than to describe my physical appearance. Physical characteristics are neutral. Once people get to know me, I trust they will judge me by my personality, my character, my mind, my sense of humor, etc. Those are the things that define me.

When Ang and I are in a place where there are few (or less) white people, it makes the most sense for me to describe her as the white woman, rather than trying to pretend that neither I nor anyone else in the room can see that she is white. Describing her in this way does not imply anything else about her. It is the simplest way to distinguish her from the other women in the room. Somewhere along the line, "they" told us that we shouldn't use the color of someone's skin to describe a person. I reject that concept. I agree that we shouldn't use skin color to *define* people, but I see no problem with using it to *describe* someone. Once we accept and make peace with the fact that we are all humans and we all bleed the same, then we can observe and celebrate our differences instead of trying to pretend we don't see them. I look forward to the day when we are all comfortable with the natural and obvious descriptions of ourselves and each other.

Until then, we need to keep in mind that, as humans, we are all going to make mistakes. Both sides share the blame for the racial awkwardness we experience in society. All of us hold preconceived notions about people of other races. These notions often lead us to believe false things and may cause us to jump to conclusions about the motives of others. Unless we acknowledge this and commit to work to make a change, we will continue to carry these biases around. That's part of being human. Our choice is whether or not we allow our humanity to continue to divide us or whether we allow it to unite us.

We are all God's children

To be clear, Christians are the target audience of this book. Just as the passage in 1 John 1:5-7 is addressing those who believe in God, we too, are making our appeal to Christians. The message of this book is primarily given to us as believers in Christ who are called to be the light of the world. Christians should be the ones leading in racial reconciliation. Jesus told us in Matthew 5:16, "In the same way, let your light shine before others, that they may see your good deeds and glorify your Father in heaven." It's time for the world to see God's people becoming a force for light and for good deeds so that God can be glorified, not only to help bring forgiveness and unity to our country (and the world), but so the world will be able to experience the true peace that comes from God.

In his book *Mission in the Old Testament: Israel as a LIGHT to the Nations*, Walter Kaiser writes about the globalization of the gospel. Kaiser asserts that God's mission was not exclusively Jewish in the Old Testament. He says, "Yahweh was truly calling all the families of the earth – even one's enemies – to the same Savior and Salvation. While Israel remains at the center of the story, this is not to say that there was not a globalization of the gospel in view."[43] This means that God's people, old and young, male and female, both Jew and Gentile, black and white, are all being sent on a mission. We are being commissioned to carry out the will of God, which is to make as many disciples as we can and to teach those disciples everything Jesus taught.

God wants everyone to experience salvation, but that is not all He wants for each person. He is also interested in the individual spiritual transformation of each of His children, for each of His followers to come to know and completely understand that His grace, love, and mercy are for them and for all nations, all races, and all people. Understanding this is a part of the discipleship process. All through the Bible, from the Old Testament through the New Testament, we can see God's intention to reach the whole world with love and grace. To accomplish this plan, He has chosen key people to bless so that they can be a blessing to everyone else. In his book *Missions in the Age of the Spirit*, author John York writes extensively about God's intention to have a redeemed people from among all nations and assigns this process the term **Missio Dei**[44] (Mission of God).

It blows my mind to think that God had all of us in mind from the beginning of time. Black people, white people, brown people—all of us! Furthermore, from the beginning of time, before any of us were born, God had a plan to redeem us and bring us into fellowship with Him. The devil knows this, and he does all that he can to stop the spread of the gospel. The Bible tells us that the enemy comes to steal, kill, and destroy.[45] It saddens me to think about all the damage the devil has been able to do through the sin of racism. It's time for God's people to say, "Enough!"

> But the fact remains

The Church needs to be the one spreading the message that we are all God's creation, that we all have the opportunity to be children of God. It has always been God's intention for those who are called by Him to demonstrate His love, forgiveness, unity, and peace.

In order for the Church to be leading the way toward racial reconciliation, each member of the Church will need to do the work of reconciling discrepancies in all areas of his or her life. This work of reconciliation has many facets. In his book *The Steward Leader*, R. Scott Rodin mentions a few of them. He teaches that we need to be reconciled to God, to ourselves, to others, and with nature. Throughout this book, we are focusing primarily on the aspect of being reconciled with others; however, we assume that reconciliation in the other areas has already taken place before reconciliation with others will be possible. Being in harmony with God facilitates being reconciled within ourselves. In order to live peacefully, we must be at peace with our own self. Rodin said, "Christ came to restore our relationship with our self and to reclaim for us a holistic understanding of who we are as his children. In Christ we are citizens of his kingdom. Even more we are children of the King!"[46]

Have you ever wanted to be royalty? Well, as a Christian, you are indeed royalty! But we aren't the type of entitled royalty who thinks life is all about us. Absolutely not! Rodin goes on to say, "As God's beloved children we have a vocation, a future and a role. We know why we are here, what our purpose is in life and where we are going.

That's what it means to be a child of God."[47] We have been restored and redeemed and given a purpose. This isn't for us only. Because of the love we have been shown, we are now being called to show this great love to other people. We have been called to the ministry of reconciliation. By redeeming our relationship to God, Jesus calls us into this right relationship with our neighbor.[48] Furthermore, we know from studying God's Word that our neighbor includes all people, even those who aren't from our tribe or our race and who don't look like us.

We are
all
God's Children

On a side note, I received several emails asking me to clarify this point. Some pointed out that we are not all God's children. They agreed that we are all God's creation but pointed out that we are not all God's children.

I understand and agree with this point of correction from a theological standpoint. Let me explain: There is a difference between being God's creation and being God's child. God created all things, which makes us all His creation.[49] Moreover, the Bible explains how it is possible to become God's child. John 1:12 in the Amplified version says, "But to as many as did receive and welcome Him, He gave the right [the authority, the privilege] to become children of God, that is, to those who believe in (adhere to, trust in, and rely on) His name." This means that all those who ask for forgiveness for their sins and invite Jesus into their heart are God's children.

You may read this book and have a hard time accepting this message of racial reconciliation and all that we are proposing—love, forgiveness, unity, and peace. It may be difficult for you to understand the concept that we are espousing, to live in the light. But yet, you keep reading because something inside of you is identifying with what we are saying. Could I suggest that God is speaking to your heart? He wants you to understand the principles we are talking about. To completely understand, however, will require that you open your heart and your mind to His ways. You can become one of His children of the light. You are only a prayer away.

The Bible teaches us that we are all sinners.[50] Every single one of us. We all miss the mark and deserve to be punished for this sin.[51] That's the dark side showing itself in our life. But it doesn't have to be this way. God made a plan for us to be set free from the darkness. He sent His son, Jesus, to die and become the ultimate sacrifice to pay our sin debt.[52] Because of His love for us, He offers to pay our debt in full. In order to take Him up on this offer to be released from the darkness, all we have to do is believe in our hearts that God raised Him from the dead and confess with our mouth that He is the Lord, and we will be saved.[53]

All of us are part of God's creation; as humans we have that in common. But, when we ask Him to come into our hearts, we move from just being in the creation category to the child category. The opportunity is available to all of us.

We have each other

When I was growing up, America was referred to as a melting pot. We were proud that our country was made up of people of all races and colors from around the world. We were taught that diversity was a good thing. However, I wonder if those lessons made their way from our heads into our hearts. It seems as though many people today view diversity as something to be feared rather than something to enjoy. Our diversity doesn't have to separate us. I believe most Americans would acknowledge this. But, getting us to the point where we appreciate and even celebrate our differences . . . well, that's another story.

Celebrating can happen when we are honest and open about the differences in the races. We are different, and we do things differently. And that's ok. It will take some getting used to, but we can do it.

Being married to a white woman for 24 years has afforded me the opportunity to learn about her family's culture. For example, I've now been to quite a few Thanksgiving dinners. And, let me tell you, "white people Thanksgiving" is different from "black people Thanksgiving." First, white people go with the traditional turkey for their main dish. It may be roasted or fried, but white folks typically have just turkey. Black people, on the other hand, usually have turkey *and* ham, fried chicken, and, to get jiggy with it, somebody typically brings some barbecued ribs!

Then, the sides. Black people have mashed potatoes and gravy, baked beans, green beans, collard greens, yams, and homemade mac and cheese that is made with real cheese baked into it. You better not bring that "mac and cheese from the box mess" to Thanksgiving dinner! We usually have corn, either on the cob or off (it doesn't matter), rolls, and grape Kool-aid. Gotta have the Kool-aid.

White people, on the other hand, will do some casseroles on Thanksgiving! I didn't know there were so many casseroles. When you go to white people Thanksgiving, you are going to have a lot of casseroles. There's green bean casserole, cornbread casserole, seven-layer-salad casserole, squash casserole, shepherd's pie casserole, cheese potato gratin (which is a cousin of casserole), and my absolute favorite—cheese and broccoli rice casserole. Oh yeah, if you are lucky, some distant aunt or cousin brings their kickin' recipe for sweet potato casserole. That stuff is bangin'! It is no exaggeration to say that at white people Thanksgiving, there may be a half dozen different kinds of casseroles in a variety of different casserole dishes. I have to admit that, until I married a white woman, I didn't even know what a casserole dish was! But, hey! I'm not complaining. White people Thanksgiving is different, but it's absolutely delicious.

There is definitely a color divide at Thanksgiving dinner and some things you will *only* get if you are at the home of one color versus the other. Like homemade noodles at white people Thanksgiving. I didn't even know that was a thing. (I thought you purchased them at the store.) I didn't know you could make noodles. Someone actually has to take the time to roll them up the day before and let them set for a while, so they are ready to cook. That's what's up! On the flip side, some black people don't think it's a Thanksgiving dinner unless someone brings some chitlins! Notice, I said "some" black people. I'm definitely not one of them. Chitlins are straight up disgusting to eat and to smell. You can always tell when you walk into a house where chitlins have been cooking. No, thank you!

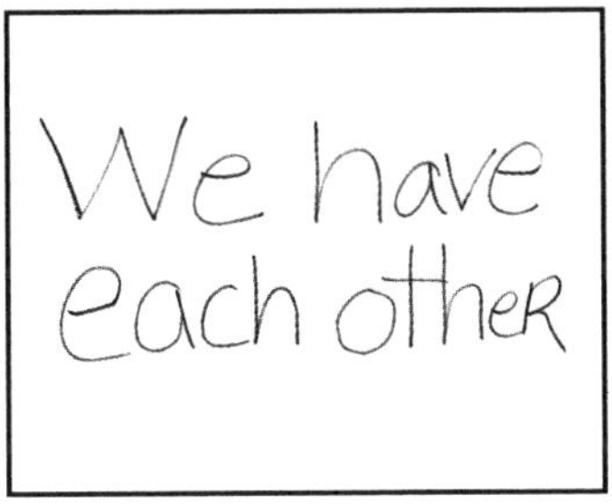

Nevertheless, the common denominator is that both black and white Thanksgiving have a lot of sharing, a lot of fun, and a lot of love. And, as our extended family has grown, we have been fortunate enough to see different races and colors at Thanksgiving dinners on either side of the family.

Our family is becoming the melting pot that represents America. Because my family gets to experience both black and white Thanksgiving dinners, we are blessed to experience it all! Friends, when we welcome and embrace each other, our blessings increase!

Now is our time

This is our time to do something to help bring about racial reconciliation. All of us can do something. Together with the actions of other like-minded people, we can create an army of people committed to Starting Again. Don't fall for the lie that one person can't really make a difference. Jesus fed thousands with the lunch of one little boy who was willing to offer up what he had. I love the following story of how one person can change the world:

> *"Once upon a time, there was an old man who used to go to the ocean to do his writing. He had a habit of walking on the beach every morning before he began*

his work. Early one morning, he was walking along the shore after a big storm had passed and found the beach littered with starfish as far as the eye could see, stretching in both directions.

Off in the distance, the old man noticed a small boy approaching. As the boy walked, he paused every so often, and, as he grew closer, the man could see that he was occasionally bending down to pick up an object and throw it into the sea. As the boy came closer, the man called out, "Good morning! May I ask what it is that you are doing?"

The young boy paused, looked up, and replied, "Throwing starfish into the ocean. The tide has washed them up onto the beach, and they can't return to the sea by themselves. When the sun gets high, they will die, unless I throw them back into the water."

The old man replied, "But there must be tens of thousands of starfish on this beach. I'm afraid you won't really be able to make much of a difference."

The boy bent down, picked up yet another starfish, and threw it as far as he could into the ocean. Then he turned, smiled, and said, "It made a difference to that one!"[54]

We all have the opportunity to help create positive change, and I believe one ordinary person can make a big difference. We are calling on Christians to act now. We need to take bold action to share the love of Christ and practice walking in fellowship with people of all races. Now is the time for the Church to rise up and take the lead by showing that we are united in our efforts for racial reconciliation. In order for true change to happen, we're going to have to do some things differently. If we are going to Start Again, Christians are going to have to demonstrate love.

When I was in college, one of my favorite music groups was DC Talk, a Christian rap group from the 1990s. They had a hit song called "Love is a Verb." The song challenged people to not just say they love others, but to show it.

> *Back in the day there was a man*
> *Who stepped out of Heaven and He walked the land*
> *He delivered to the people an eternal choice*
> *With a heart full of luv and the truth in His voice*
> *Gave up His life so that we may live*
> *How much more luv could the Son of God give?*
> *Here is the example that we oughtta be matchin'*
> *Cause luv is a word that requires some action*[55]

Don't just say you love people, show your love! The Church has to do a better job of showing people of all races that we love them. Love requires action. Now is the time for us to take the lead in striving for racial unity. At the end of this book, we will offer a few suggestions of things you can do to put love into action when it comes to racial reconciliation. However, why don't you take the time right now to think about a few things you can do to show love to people of other races? Let's Start Again by making love a verb. After all, we are all in this together, and everyone needs a little more love!

Who Are We Becoming?

CHAPTER EIGHT

"Racism comes in many different forms. Sometimes it's subtle, and sometimes it's overt. Sometimes it's violent, and sometimes it's harmless, but it's definitely here. It's something that I think we're all guilty of, and we just have to make sure that we deal with our own personal racism in the right way."
– Jordan Peele

8

Who are We? Who are We Becoming?

Martin Luther King, Jr. once said, "Let no man pull you low enough to hate him." Let me tell you a real-life story of a friend of mine who epitomizes this. She and I grew up in the same small town in Illinois, and I've known her pretty much all of my life. She understands what it's like to be the only black kid in your class and one of only a handful of black kids in your school. Like me, she grew up around white people and has a very positive view of race relations in America. She works two jobs as a traveling nurse practitioner. One clinic is in St. Louis, where she primarily sees black patients. However, the other job is in a rural clinic in Kentucky that serves mostly white patients. She works weekends and is the primary health care provider on those days.

One day at the clinic in Kentucky, the nurses informed my friend that there was a patient scheduled to see her. But, they added, they would understand if she didn't want to see him. He was an older white gentleman who frequented the clinic. They knew him to be a proud supporter of the Aryan Nations. He openly displayed his tattoo supporting the neo-Nazi, white supremacist, terrorist organization. Her white coworkers were offended for her because of this man's blatant racism so boldly displayed. My friend politely thanked them for their concern and indicated that she was open to seeing all patients who came in for care. She walked into his exam room and began to give him the same quality of care that she was accustomed to giving to people who look like her in St. Louis. She had decided in her heart that she wasn't going to let this man's racist beliefs change her or affect how she treated him.

She gave him excellent service, displaying her kind and caring nature in every move she made. She was so kind that at the end of the exam, he made mention of the elephant in the room. He asked her why she was being so nice to him under the circumstances. She told her patient she was committed to caring for all people and spreading love to all of her patients, no matter their race, and no matter what they might think of her. By the end of her time serving him, this obviously racist gentleman apologized to my black nurse practitioner friend and kindly thanked her for her service.

My friend demonstrates abandoning the mindset that has kept us divided. Instead of showing him the same attitude of hate and division he displayed, she was determined to be the light in this dark situation.

We are calling for each of us to take an introspective look and examine who we have become. Have you succumbed to the narrative from the media and vocal minority that says, "Stay in your corner" or, "They can't be trusted?" It's time for black and white Christians to *unite* and to bring positive change to our communities, to lead our country and the rest of the world to racial reconciliation. The Church needs to lead the way. It's time to become who God created us to be.

In contrast to my nurse practitioner friend, I recently had a conversation with three young tattoo artists from Atlanta, Georgia, who were each in their early 30's. We talked about the issues we have with race in our country. They gave me a few stories about run-ins they have had with the police and expressed their feelings of intense distrust toward any police officer, of any color, even to the point of hatred.

One of the young men talked about the epidemic of police killing unarmed black men. He talked about how he felt unsafe walking around the streets of Atlanta and he didn't trust the police at all. Although I understand their sentiments and realize many black and brown people feel that way, I was shocked at their visceral disdain toward the police. I shared with them how I endeavored to teach my kids to be respectful of the police, conveying to them that I have several family members who are police officers. I pushed back on the view that all police officers are bad and gave examples of positive interactions I've had with cops. I talked about how mutual respect could help restore the relationship between the police and the people. The same young man expressed to me that he didn't have any respect for police officers. "I don't say 'Yes, Sir' and 'No, Sir' to anyone!" He agreed when I told him this could potentially lead him into trouble. His response: "So be it!"

The three men went on to talk about how the police are power hungry and treat all people harshly, especially black and brown people who don't look like them. One of the guys said he understood this power-hungry mindset. He went on to tell me about the first time he held a gun in his hand when he was a teenager. He instantly realized he had a new source of power, and his first thought was to display this power by going out and robbing someone.

I was shocked. Although some can identify with this point of view, I can't. Why was this his first thought? I've heard others say they, too, felt this sense of power the first time they held a gun in their hand, but why did he want to use this power to commit a crime? To rob someone? Unfortunately, he has been conditioned to believe power and violence go hand in hand. This is a huge mistake. A quick glance across America confirms he is not alone in this belief. I have spoken with several black people who feel the same way as these young men from Atlanta. They feel a deep distrust and animosity toward the police that traces back many years.

The movie *Straight Outta Compton* tells the story of the impact that the 1990s rap group NWA had on culture. NWA's music was full of stories of young black men being harassed by police and the brutality they dealt with growing up in South Central California. They had a defiant attitude and boldly proclaimed they weren't going to take being racially profiled, harassed, or mistreated. Many black people from all over America identified with them, which contributed to their popularity. Their 1988 hit song, "F tha Police," is a protest song they wrote for their album *Straight Outta Compton*. Decades later, their message is still embraced by many people. This song was ranked number 425 on Rolling Stone's list of the 500 Greatest Songs of All Time.[56]

Black people have felt marginalized and mistreated in America for years. Our civil rights leaders took heavy physical blows in order to gain the freedoms we have now. Some among us grew weary of the peaceful approach and decided to gain justice and equality by any means necessary, even violence. Generations later, some black people still hold to the notion that since we were oppressed and abused for so long, it's now our turn to be the oppressor. Sadly, this has led to acts of violence towards all people, not just those who have perpetrated racist activity. Violence and crime within our own communities are byproducts of this violent mindset. We have seen the damaging effects of this in our own neighborhoods and cities, which are plagued with high crime, low-paying jobs, low home values, and urban decay. We have to abandon this mindset, which only further perpetuates the stereotype of black people being criminals. It is understandable that people want to push back against those who they feel are responsible for their oppression. I understand being fed up to the point where you feel you need to fight. However, in the struggle for justice and equality, we would be wise to strive for progress, not revenge.

At the same time, police need to acknowledge that black and brown people have been policed differently than white people throughout history, and, sadly, still are today in many areas. For example, we saw this firsthand while living in St. Louis in regards to traffic light cameras. In certain places in the city, traffic cameras were used to ensure that traffic laws were being obeyed. A person would receive a $100 ticket in the mail if they ran a red light or made an illegal right turn. These cameras were prevalent in black communities. Whenever I would drive into the city, I was in danger of getting one of these tickets. At a certain intersection, a tiny sign was posted that said you were allowed to turn right on a red light, but only during specific times. (I may or may not have gotten seven of these tickets in less than six months. I can neither confirm nor deny!) However, in the area we lived, a suburb south of the city, we didn't have traffic cameras. (Neither did the suburbs and areas west of the city.) Interestingly enough, these were predominantly white parts of St. Louis. Black people in St. Louis noticed this injustice, and this played a part in diminishing their trust of police and the legal justice system. Police officers need to acknowledge prejudice in their hearts and minds and the racism inherent in our legal system and demonstrate a change in their attitude and behavior toward our communities of color. Respect is a two-way street and is always better earned rather than assumed or demanded.

White Privilege

This seems as good a time as any to address the subject of White Privilege. It's one of those phrases that sends chills up our spines. For many black people, it reminds them of the discrepancies and injustices they encounter on a regular basis. For white people, it often brings about feelings of frustration, because many of them do not consider the hardworking middle class (or lower) life they lead to be one filled with much privilege. Some have gone so far as to say that the term is a myth. Angie had the chance to discuss this issue with a high school classmate. It all started over a social media post regarding her friend's perception of white privilege. Here's Angie's account of what happened:

I was scrolling through my newsfeed one day and came across a video that promised to debunk the concept of white privilege. A young man was speaking on a college campus and shared his perspective of how white privilege is a myth. Well, that quickly caught my attention, and, as I looked to see who had posted this video, I was actually surprised that it was my old classmate. Coming from a small, rural, Midwestern community, I was not shocked that something like this might appear in my newsfeed, but that this particular friend shared the post did surprise me. This friend is someone whom I have always considered to be very open minded and liberal in his worldview. In fact, he and I never saw eye to eye as high school classmates. A few of our mutual friends chimed in to express their "like" of the subject matter. Again, I was shocked. But, as I read my friend's reason for posting the video, I began to understand that he had been discriminated against because he is white. He felt frustrated and wanted to point out that just because you're white doesn't mean that everything works out well for you. He and I were able to have a great conversation about this issue, and he gave me permission to share it with you. I'm very thankful for that, because it is a great example of how people can have completely different opinions and yet create a safe space to discuss issues in an intelligent and cordial way. Here is the conversation taken straight off his social media account.

My Friend: *Several years ago I called to complain about the offensive actions of a coworker only to literally be told, "because you're a white male, and not a 'protected class,' nothing will be done. Have a nice day." I have worked for everything I have. Made choices and sacrifices. My mother did the same. The idea that I have it better because of my skin color is racist.*

Me: *There is no doubt that you have worked hard for everything you have. And it sounds like your experience with being told that, since you were not a minority your concern was invalid was handled terribly. BUT, those things don't prove that white privilege is a myth. White privilege is very much a real thing. I see it when I'm given excellent customer service when I am alone and tell my husband how nice people are at the eye doctor's office and then when he takes our kids in the same lady is rude and disrespectful to him.*

Maybe she isn't a racist person, but maybe she just feels more comfortable around other white people. Or maybe she was having a bad day. I see it when my husband and I drive through small towns and he gets pulled over for no reason (after we had just momentarily had the dome light on). And, I get the "Ma'am, are you sure you are alright"? Have you ever had a lady in your car when you got pulled over and had the officer ask her that? Or when my husband does get pulled over in a small town for driving a few miles over the speed limit and we worry that he might end up in jail, or worse, through no fault of his own. I saw it when I got called a "nigger lover" in our home town for simply being seen with my friend (at the time) at Hardee's the night before. I see it when I decide whether or not I should marry the man of my dreams because by doing so I might be disowned by my Southern belle grandmother whose family (just a few generations back) owned slaves.

None of these are hypothetical examples and none of them are things white people usually have to deal with or even ever think about. Yes, we all get treated unfairly sometimes, but, black people really do have a few extra strikes against them just because of the color of their skin. If we are being honest, we have to acknowledge that white people really don't get discriminated against in the same way black people do. Is it really so unfair that there is such a thing as Black History Month or BET? I mean, we don't have White History Month or White Entertainment Television? It's because we are the majority culture. Our culture is represented all over the place! If we hadn't had hundreds of years of slavery and then segregation then we would not have had two drastically different cultures. But, we did and now we do. Us white people really truly had all the power at one time. That really does trickle down and have repercussions still to this day. We have to be honest and aware of that. But we shouldn't feel bad about being white either. And, discriminating against white people in 2018 doesn't fix the problem of injustices from the past.

But, let's face it, it is a rare occasion where black people have the authority to discriminate against white people in our day-to-day interactions anyway.

The guy in this video is so divisive and seems to be so very hateful and angry. Nobody rights wrongs with that type of attitude.

I just wish we could get to the place where we see Dr. King's dream fulfilled. Where people would just be kind and considerate and treat each other, individually, not by the color of their white or black skin, but by the content of their character. Anytime we start looking at any situation from an us against them mentality there will always be a winner and loser. In my family, we don't get the "privilege" of picking a side. And honestly, I think that's a good thing.

So, I sent my friend that message and wondered how it would be received. I got a sweet response back from him:

My friend: *Angela, I hope my post from a few days ago didn't offend you. I really really appreciate your comments, and thoughtful dialogue. I feel that you are very brave to say the things you said. My intent is never to offend anyone. I agree with you that the guy is a little too pointed in his remarks. I wish that race was never an issue and we could all embrace each other for who they are inside.*

Me: *I really appreciate you following up about this. And, thank-you for your kind words. I was really surprised you posted it because I've always thought of you as being a really open-minded, tolerant person. And, on the other hand, I kind of laughed about the fact that we never did see eye to eye when we were kids! I'm not offended. Because, even though I didn't like that you posted it and indicated that you liked it, I expected/hoped you would respond to my reaction to it just like you have. I probably would have been offended if things had gone south after my response. I think you're a pretty great guy, just like I think my Grandma was a great woman and lots of other great people who aren't aware of their own prejudices and the reality of racism in our country. I never once felt that you had ill intent towards me or Alex, and yet, I hope you now see how it could come across* *that way. I think the biggest struggle we have in dealing with racism is that most of us just don't have any meaningful relationships outside our race. The issues don't ever actually hit home. As long as we stay in our white world, we don't ever see racism. Well, yeah, race isn't an issue when you don't have to interact with people of other races. It isn't personal until there is an actual person you care about involved. And then it can't not be personal.*

Our lives are connected

Friends, people really can make a difference, one conversation at a time, one small step toward living in the light at a time. It's time for us to do away with the divisive mindset.

Our country has been divided for far too long. We have to free the next generation to think about their future. Those coming along behind us can see things from a different, unified perspective. We can Start Again! We do this by demonstrating to the next generation a better way.

Changes

Tupac tried to teach this to our community when he wrote the song "Changes" way back in 1992. In this song, he deals with a lot of cultural issues of the time—the war on drugs, the treatment of black people by the police, and racism. The lyrics of this song and the message of reconciliation between the races in America is still relevant today. His lyrics are deep . . .

> *We under I wonder what it takes to make this*
> *One better place, let's erase the wasted*
> *Take the evil out the people they'll be acting right*
> *'Cause both black and white is smokin' crack tonight*
> *And only time we chill is when we kill each other*
> *It takes skill to be real, time to heal each other*

Tupac wrote about what was really happening in urban America, and the people in those communities listened to him because he was telling their truth. He spoke about the perpetuation of poverty and its accompanying vicious cycle value system in urban African-American culture. He spoke about the difficulties of life in the ghetto.

But some things will never change
Try to show another way but you stayin' in the dope game
Now tell me what's a mother to do
Bein' real don't appeal to the brother in you
You gotta operate the easy way
"I made a G today" But you made it in a sleazy way
Sellin' crack to the kid. " I gotta get paid,"
Well hey, well that's the way it is

The thing about Tupac is that he saw the need to do what he could to break this vicious cycle. He challenged black and brown people to take responsibility for wrong actions, to educate ourselves to live a better way, and to make changes! He was challenging black people to take personal responsibility for our actions and our futures. This is completely different from the victim mindset that many espouse today. He goes on to say . . .

We gotta make a change
It's time for us as a people to start makin' some changes.
Let's change the way we eat, let's change the way we live
And let's change the way we treat each other.
You see the old way wasn't working so it's on us to do
What we gotta do, to survive.

Real change will happen when enough of us realize that the old way isn't working, and we have to make changes in order to survive. We have a choice about who we are becoming. We are either going to unite in love and in the light or continue down the path of darkness and disunity.

Our natural tendency is to feel more comfortable around people who look like us, speak like us, and come from the same background that we come from. Although this is a natural tendency, we must learn to be comfortable around people who don't look like us or who aren't from our race, nationality, or tribe. As we said, the old way isn't working. We must be committed to doing better—being better. This must happen on all sides. We must intentionally place ourselves around people of other races. Over time, we will find that we see a change in our comfort zone.

As Angie and I have reflected about who we are and who we are becoming, we've decided to share some of our stories that show the journey we've been on. Here's one of mine:

Who are we? Who are we becoming?

I once lived in a neighborhood for about five years with a neighbor I assumed I wouldn't really jive with. He was older, didn't talk much, chain smoked, and had two big dogs (the kind that could have eaten any of my kids in a single bite) that he frequently took for walks in the neighborhood. We were at different points in life . . . .

He was retired with no kids in the house. My thought process was this: Most retired people don't want to be around families with young kids. The kids will lose balls in their yard and just annoy them with never-ending noise and chatter. Furthermore, he was an older white guy who probably didn't approve of interracial marriages. I could just see him turning his nose up and thinking that his property value dropped because there's now a black man in the neighborhood with his n$&@!-loving wife.

He chain smoked! Cigarette after cigarette, so even when I tried to engage him in a quick conversation, the smoke was just more than I could bear. I mean, who wants to be outside of your house and come back in smelling like smoke?

He didn't talk much. So, I didn't say much to him, either. Then, just weeks before Christmas one year, I noticed he started to drop a lot of weight - fast! I quickly recognized that his situation wasn't good. I had lost a grandmother to cancer and had two uncles battling cancer at the time, all from chain smoking. But, I didn't say anything to him. At that point, it would seem like I was just being nosy. I convinced myself that it would be rude to start asking questions and pretending like I was interested in his life. So, I said nothing. As the weeks progressed, I noticed he didn't walk the dogs anymore and didn't work in his yard. As a matter of fact, the only thing I would see him do was sit in a chair at the edge of the garage watching people go by.

I knew I had to go and talk to him. But, after five years, how would I be received? Finally, I decided I had to pay him a visit.

It was about 11:00 p.m., and I saw his garage light on while I was taking out my garbage. I decided to go over and talk with him. It was very awkward because, as I crossed the street and entered his yard, I realized I didn't even know his name. I thought I had heard him being called "Skip" before, but I wasn't sure. So, I had to wing it. I started with small talk, "nice weather, beautiful night, spring is here..." But it wasn't long before I brought up the obvious. I said I hadn't seen him out as much, and it looked like he had lost a lot of weight. I asked how his health was. He gave the answer that I already knew—cancer. Lung cancer. Radiation, chemo, very little hope.

At that moment I realized that between the two of us, there really was only one bad neighbor! I felt so ashamed and convicted as we sat there and talked, while he openly revealed private details of his life as if we had been friends for years. Not only was he extremely open, but he was very gracious and generous in excusing my poor efforts to reach out and be neighborly. We talked for about 30 minutes that night, and I told him I wanted to pray for him before I left. I proudly exclaimed to him that I was a pastor (as if this statement would reassure him that my occupation gave my prayers a more direct line to God or something), and he said, "I know you are a pastor," and smiled. I felt even more ashamed.

I had read the book Just Walk Across the Room *by Bill Hybels. He challenges each of us to pray for and make attempts to witness to our neighbors and win them to Christ. When I finished this book, I walked around my neighborhood and boldly prayed for some of my neighbors to come to know Jesus—the ones I thought were ready and open to Him. To my shame, this neighbor wasn't even on the list.*

All that time, I stayed on my side of the street thinking I lived next to a really bad neighbor, when, in reality, the terrible neighbor was me! Don't be a bad neighbor like me. God calls us to go everywhere and tell everyone about His Son. This includes telling the people across the street. Let's be about the Father's business!

Being about our Father's business. That's the example Jesus gave. *We*, the Church, have allowed race to divide us for far too long. The answer to the question "Who are we becoming?" should be: Like Jesus. We should be becoming like Jesus. Sharing His light and love with *everyone*!

CHAPTER NINE

The Two Sides are Dark versus Light

"There is neither Jew nor Gentile, neither slave nor free, nor is there male and female, for you are all one in Christ Jesus" (Galatians 3:28, NIV).

9

The Two Sides are Dark versus Light

I love the Star Wars movies. All of them! I remember being in grade school when the first one came out, and I immediately fell in love with Darth Vader. I know he was the bad guy and all, but something about him was so stinkin' cool. His outfit: dressed in all black with a cool, flowing cape. His walk: he walked with a swagger, never in a hurry but always right on time. His theme music: you can play those few notes almost anywhere in the world, and people will think of Darth Vader. His mastery of using the power of the force! Millions of kids walked around doing fake air chokes to their siblings. And then, the breathing . . . the voice . . . James Earl Jones. Although he was the villain, I found myself rooting for him. Darth Vader was the man!

Then, in the second movie, "The Empire Strikes Back," that's when I became a full-fledged Darth Vader fan! Two movies led up to this famous, iconic scene . . . Darth Vader uses the dark side of the force to beckon Luke to the final battle. Luke enters the scene, and Vader appears abruptly, and they begin to fight with their lightsabers. Luke strikes first, but he's no match for Vader, who is strong in the dark side of the force. Vader overpowers Luke and cuts off his hand, sending his lightsaber into the abyss. Luke crawls away, and, instead of killing him, Vader invites him to join him on the Dark Side. Then Darth Vader drops some knowledge on Luke . . .

Darth Vader: *There is no escape! Don't make me destroy you. Luke, you do not yet realize your importance. You've only begun to discover your power! Join me, and I will complete your training! With our combined strength, we can end this destructive conflict and bring order to the galaxy.*

Luke Skywalker: *[angrily] I'll never join you!*

Vader: *If only you knew the power of the Dark Side. Obi-Wan never told you what happened to your father.*

Luke: *He told me enough! He told me you killed him!*

Vader: *No, I am your father.*

Luke: *[shocked] No. No! That's not true! That's impossible!*

Vader: *Search your feelings; you know it to be true!*

Luke: *NOOOOOOO! NOOOOOOOO!!!*

That scene was awesome! I watched it as a boy and couldn't wait to share it with my kids when they were old enough. I can remember my third son, Mason, really getting into the Star Wars series, so we watched all the movies together, forty years after I saw the original one. We watched them in Episode order, starting with the later-released Episodes I, II, and III. I wanted him to see the story in timeline order from start to finish. I'm so glad we did, because Mason knew about Darth Vader but didn't really know much about his backstory. So, by the time we came to Episode V, "The Empire Strikes Back," and when it came to the end scene where Vader reveals he is Luke's father, Mason lets out a loud, "Yes! I knew it!" I think Vader is his favorite character, too (dark side and all).

I've often wondered what it is about the Dark Side that draws us to it. Perhaps it's because deep down inside of all of us, there is a dark side to contend with. The Bible has a lot to say about this, warning us to be aware of the evil and darkness lurking inside each of us, starting with our heart. The Bible says the human heart is the most deceitful of all things and desperately wicked.[57] It's hard to understand what is in our heart and how it got there.

In their book *Overcoming the Dark Side of Leadership*, Gary L. McIntosh and Samuel D. Rima said that everyone has a dark side; it's just part of our natural human development.[58] This was reassuring to hear. No one wants to feel alone or like they are evil because they have a dark side. It's important to understand that this is natural. However, what we do with it, either allowing it to negatively affect us or dealing with it, is the important thing. McIntosh and Rima go on to suggest, "We redeem our dark side and learn to deal with it so that it turns into something useful and life giving."

This would suggest that we have no one to blame for our dark side, other than ourselves, not even the devil. We are the ones to blame for our wrong actions that come out as a result of the negative influence of not dealing with our dark side.

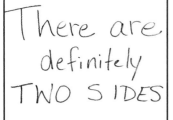

There are definitely TWO SIDES

The Bible teaches that all of us are born sinful.[59] We all have a dark side that needs to be redeemed. When we view racism as a sin, an evil and wicked sin that spreads hate, we realize that we are all born with the propensity to succumb to the sin of racism.

Many people have observed that racism is learned; it is not innate. They say children are born with love in their heart and are willing to share love with anyone regardless of color. Unfortunately, the sin of racism keeps being passed from one generation to the next, the sins of the fathers visiting their children, so to speak.

The results of any one of us leaving our dark side unchecked can be felt by all of us. We've seen this play out time and time again in the

United States. Most recently, on the morning of Saturday, August 3, 2019, in El Paso, Texas, just after 10:35 a.m., a 21-year-old gunman armed with a powerful rifle turned a crowded Walmart store in this majority-Hispanic border city into a scene of chaos and bloodshed. The gunman stalked shoppers in the aisles in an attack that left 22 people dead and 24 others wounded. He wrote a manifesto on an anti-immigrant online website titled "The Inconvenient Truth." This manifesto outlines fears about Hispanic people gaining power in the United States.

And again, less than 24 hours later, in Dayton, Ohio, our nation woke to the news of another mass shooting. While most of us were sleeping, at 1:07 a.m., a shooter killed nine people and injured 26 others in less than a minute. It happened in a busy neighborhood full of bars and restaurants where "thousands of people" usually gather on a summer Saturday night to have fun. The Mayor of Dayton, Nan Whaley, suggested the death toll would have been much higher if the police hadn't already been in the district at the time. Counting these two incidents, in the first eight months of this year, there have been over 250 mass shootings in the US, which have seen more than 520 people killed and over 2,000 people injured. A mass shooting is defined as "an incident in which four or more people are shot or killed." That's a lot of darkness!

The Truth is . . .

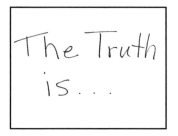

The Dark Side:
Fear leads to Anger
Anger leads to Hate
Hate leads to Suffering

FEAR: People are afraid of what they don't know. The shooter in El Paso was afraid that people who don't look like him were coming in to take over America. His fear was irrational, but it is a fear nonetheless.

ANGER:
When we give in to our fears of what "they" are doing, we begin to believe the lies of the enemy that come to divide and conquer us.

HATRED: Anger externalized causes people to do things like devise a plan to walk into Walmart and start shooting black or brown people.

SUFFERING: It's obvious to see how much suffering has taken place. Too many mothers have lost their black and brown sons. Too many people have combed through social media accounts looking for the words "Marked Safe" from yet another incident of racially-motivated violence.

We have to take action in order to overcome the darkness! McIntosh and Rima offer practical steps for us to utilize when redeeming our dark side. The first thing they suggest is that we admit and acknowledge our dark side. When we admit our shortcomings, we are acknowledging we need God's grace to help us. Second, they suggest we examine our past so we will be able to know how to deal with the dark side.[60] We are the sum of the experiences in our lives. The purpose for examining the past is not to blame others, but for self-examination. And, finally, we have to truly understand and accept our identity in Christ. This is the message we continue to reinforce:

"This is the message we have heard from him and declare to you: God is light; in him there is no darkness at all. If we claim to have fellowship with him and yet walk in the darkness, we lie and do not live out the truth. But if we walk in the light, as he is in the light, we have fellowship with one another, and the blood of Jesus, his Son, purifies us from all sin." 1 John 1:5-7 [61]

Christians are being asked to live as children of the light, to live out the truth that God is love, that in Him is no darkness at all. It's time for us to stand up to our dark side so that we can let the light shine through us. We have to decide if we want to be good or evil. And then do good things so others can see. Maybe they will then be inspired to do good things, too. The wisest man to have ever walked the earth said, "Good people do good things because of the good in their hearts, but bad people do bad things because of the evil in their hearts. Your words show what is in your heart."[62]

We have to drive the darkness out and let the love of Jesus and the spread of the Gospel be what we focus on. And the good news of the Gospel is Jesus died so that everyone could receive forgiveness of their sins.

> It's
> Dark vs Light
> not
> Black vs White

The 1st John passage informs us that the blood of Jesus will purify us from all sin, which will lead to us having fellowship with one another; this includes people of all races. Receiving forgiveness is the way forward. This is the message that the Church has to continue to relay to the world. To be clear, God sent us on a mission to tell the world about Jesus, who is the one Person who can purify us and unify us and set us on the right path. And nothing, not even the sin of racism, should distract us from our mission.

God's Mission for the Church

From the beginning of time, God intended for all nations and races to be united in pursuing Him. God called Abraham to "go" and promised that through him all nations would be blessed. When Jesus instructed His followers to "go and make disciples of all nations," in Matthew 28:19,[63] He was not giving a new mandate, but rather a continuation of His call. From the Old Testament to the New Testament, it has been God's intention to reach the whole world with love and grace. It was always God's plan for all people to be redeemed. Jesus reiterated this by giving instructions to His Church to go and make disciples of all nations. Unfortunately, the sin of racism has been one of the most effective tools the enemy has used to distract the Church from its mission. Sadly, he has been using this tool for centuries.

In his book, *Fire From Heaven*, Harvey Cox offered an extensive history of the Azusa Street Revival, the start of Pentecostalism in the United States, and explained the role racism played in determining how Pentecostals organized and structured themselves afterward. Cox says, "It's impossible to understand Pentecostal origins without reference to the story of one particular man. That man is William Joseph Seymour, a black preacher born in 1870 of parents who were former slaves in Centerville, Louisiana."[64] Seymour led people of all races, genders, and social classes in seeking after the Lord in spirit and in truth. It's disappointing to see how racism played a part in ending this divine outpouring of the Holy Spirit and later how it divided the leaders who organized the movements formed from the Azusa Street outpouring. Even though the Holy Spirit did a supernatural work of bringing people together, the sin of racism was successful in dividing the Church. In his article entitled "A Rhetorical History of Race Relations in the Early Pentecostal Movement," Erik Hjalmeby says, "William Seymour had a transcendent message of unity, which resulted in an unprecedented integration of all races in the middle of a segregated and racially stratified society."[65] Author Frank Bartleman reported that color lines were washed away by the blood. It is disappointing to learn how some white church leaders later attempted to discredit and shame Seymour and all that happened at Azusa Street.

Consider for a moment just how unique this move of God at Azusa Street truly was. This was the turn of the 20th century, and racism ruled supreme in all corners of the country. However, at Azusa, those lines of separation vanished. In his article, "How Azusa Street Exposed and Overturned Racism in the Church," Daniel K. Norris says, "William Seymour was overseeing something that defied reason. People from all different walks of life were coming together to participate in this revival. It is one of the truly remarkable and uncelebrated phenomenon of Azusa. In many ways it could be considered the first civil rights movement of the 1900s and it started in a multi-racial prayer meeting!"[66] People of all walks of life, black, white, and Asian, all gathered together in unity, just to pray. From this, revival broke out, and the Pentecostal movement was introduced to America. From this multi ethnic prayer meeting, God equipped the Church for the spread of the Gospel to move forth in a supernatural way.

God's people, both Jew and Gentile, black and white, are being sent on a mission. They are being commissioned to carry out the will of God, to make disciples and teach those disciples everything Jesus taught.[67] Furthermore every disciple of Christ is called to make other disciples of people of all nations and all races. Modern day Missio Dei. God is not only interested in salvation for all His children, but He is interested in the individual spiritual transformation of each of His children as well. His will is for all of His followers to come to know and completely understand that His grace, love, and mercy are not only for them, but for all nations. He wants all people to be connected to Him and then to be a part of sharing His message of love, forgiveness, unity, and peace.

The Dark Side:
Fear leads to Anger
leads to Hate
leads to Suffering

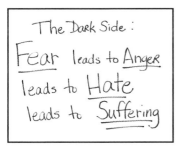

But not everyone sees it this way. The church in America is guilty of being silent and going along with the same racist and segregated actions prevalent in society during key periods of time.

Throughout American history, the Church perpetuated this view and was complicit in painting Jesus as a white man. Many white Americans assumed that "being Christian" meant that people of other races would assume the values and norms of the majority race. Some objected when ethnic minorities sought to learn more about their own heritage and focus much of their effort on bettering their own people. In an article called, "Whitewashed Christianity," Ernest Cleo Grant II said: "As lovers of Jesus who are unified by His atoning work, we cannot define unity in terms that suppress rather than welcome brothers and sisters into discovering their cultural heritage. As Christians, when we recognize the credence of other ethnicities and the value of their distinctive customs, lifestyles, and particularly their economic and political beliefs, it causes us to appreciate God-using them as agents of gospel witnesses in their communities."[68] As a part of discipleship, we must all make room for different races to seek God in their own way, according to their own culture, and be accepting of people wanting to help their own communities. Historically, the American Church has not demonstrated that they are comfortable with this type of diversity.

Church, while we were asleep at the wheel, being distracted by the differences in worship styles, or whatever excuses we made to not be a diverse and unified body, people have literally been gunned down outside our walls. We *must* be about our Father's business: the business of making disciples. We must be people who lay aside personal preferences and love like Jesus loves; red and yellow, black and white, they are precious in His sight.

The parallels between the way God intended the world to be and the universe that George Lucas created are crazy! Allow me to point out just a few. Both tell the story of good versus evil. Both settings take place on earth and in galaxies and realms far far away. And both are full of characters and creatures that expand our imagination. What in the world is a leviathan? The Bible mentions this creature five times.[69] Have you ever seen one? For all the other Star Wars fans like me, you had to be mesmerized by all the different creatures and characters that George Lucas introduced in the movie series: Chewbacca, R2-D2, C-3PO, Darth Maul, Jar Jar Binks, Jabba the Hut, Count Dooku, and who could forget the lovable Ewoks. Some of these characters were good and some were evil.

Of all those good characters, the one I admire the most is Yoda. When we are first introduced to him, we see him as a wise older member of the Jedi, one who has mastered the use of the Force. There are many life lessons we can learn from Jedi Master Yoda, and many people have heard me share some of his wise teachings throughout the years . . .

"Do or do not, there is no try."

"Your feelings will betray you . . . "

"Always pass along what you have learned."

But perhaps his best lesson and greatest piece of advice is when he warns about the path to the dark side. He's the one who said fear leads to anger, and anger leads to hate, and hate leads to suffering. He warned Darth Vader about the draw of the dark side when he was a young man, but unfortunately Vader didn't listen. He gave in to his fear, fear of losing the one he loved. Then his fear turned into hatred after he ended up losing the one he loved, by his own doing, I might add. (You really need to see the movies). Then, well, I'm sure you have at least heard about all the suffering Darth Vader caused. All of this could have been prevented had he listened to Yoda's warning to avoid giving into the dark side. In fact, he was warned to not even entertain those wicked thoughts. It's too late for Vader, but not for us. You and I, my friends, can heed Yoda's advice. Instead of choosing the dark side and giving in to fear, hate, and suffering, let's choose to walk in the light.

It Doesn't Have to be This Way

There is an expectation among most Christians that, socially, they will be accepting of all people – including those of other races. Sadly, this doesn't always happen. Prejudice, bigotry, and racism is just as prevalent within the Church as it is outside the Church walls. This shouldn't be. Christians should lead the way in racial reconciliation. Unfortunately, too many Christians avoid addressing this issue.

After Azusa Street, the Church became increasingly segregated which has negatively affected discipleship efforts. The trend is for the Church to be segregated based on race. Black people are with their own, whites are with their own, and brown people do their own thing. Each congregation sings, preaches, dresses, eats and fellowships in the way they feel most comfortable. Congregational segregation is masked when church leaders explain the reason for the lack of diversity within their congregations as a personal preference issue. This view is drastically hindering our discipleship efforts within the church. Churches are segregated by race. It's been said that the 10 o'clock hour of Sunday morning is the most segregated hour of every week.

Racism has been allowed to hide inside the Church for too long. Whether leaders are afraid to address it, unaware it exists, or don't know what to say or do, the effects of it are causing individual believers to view their brothers and sisters in Christ differently. Dr. Ernest Grant believes the Church has to be purged of the sin of racism that is mainly seen in isolationism and segregationism.[70] Too many Christians are comfortable with going to a church that suits their preferences of music, activities, and race.

Discipleship is the mission that Christians are called to. When the sin of racism is allowed to divide us, we will not effectively fulfill the mission to which God has called us. By allowing segregated churches to be the norm, the Church is allowing this sin to prevail. This has caused hatred, bitterness, anger, and division among the Church far too long. One reason for this breakdown in discipleship is because pastors reason that different people prefer different styles, therefore church services do not include aspects to attract more racial diversity to worship services. This isn't done maliciously or even purposefully, but it is happening, nonetheless. And, it's being done by all cultures, black, white, brown, and many other people groups. Leaders of all races are unwittingly continuing to perpetuate segregated congregations among the Lord's Church by allowing personal preference to trump biblical teaching.

The Church must wake up and realize this is a problem and then change how we operate. The regression of Pentecostalism, away from its diverse roots, toward a more homogeneous worldview is a problem. It is visually seen in the absence of diversity within church congregations and is felt by the level of racism and bigotry experienced in the nation and within the church walls.

Spiritually speaking, God blesses people who dwell together in unity. From the Old Testament to the New Testament, the Bible has plenty to say about racial equality and unity. Psalms 133:1 says; "Behold, how good and pleasant it is when brothers dwell in unity!"[71] According to various versions of this passage, God expects His children to live together in unity, harmony, peace, and as one. At a time of immense racial and gender inequality in Scripture, God spoke to Joel and promised that anyone and everyone who calls on His name can be a part of His family.[72]

Malachi 2:10 asks the question: "Do we not all have one father? Has not one God created us?"[73] Subsequently, Paul identified with the theme of racial unity when he said to the church in Galatia: "There is neither Jew nor Greek, there is neither slave nor free, there is no male and female, for you are all one in Christ Jesus."[74]

Similarly, John the Revelator gave a glimpse of what heaven will look like when he said: "After this I looked, and behold, a great multitude that no one could number, from every nation, from all tribes and peoples and languages, standing before the throne and before the Lamb,[75] clothed in white robes, with palm branches in their hands, and crying out with a loud voice, 'Salvation belongs to our God who sits on the throne, and to the Lamb!'"

I love this! Heaven will house people from every nation, tribe, race, and color. The Church needs to ask itself what kind of disciples are being produced. If the races are allowed to stay segregated, does this produce the type of disciples who will be ready for a diverse heaven?

An aspect of God's image is missing when we are not diverse. Just as the body consists of various parts all working together to achieve different things, Christians of various races, groupings, and undertakings need to unite to achieve the tasks God set forth to be accomplished. God created the world to be full of diverse people and He intends for all to unite under the banner of His son, Jesus. God gave everyone different skills and strengths so we each would recognize the need for one another and appreciate each other's individuality.

Unity calls for a new way of thinking. God intends for His people to come together. He didn't make humanity different so that people could be subjugated because of race, ability, or experiences. A hatred for diversity doesn't reflect a love for the One who created everything to be diverse. The Church should talk about these cultural and racial differences and celebrate them because this is what makes each person uniquely beautiful and useful to fulfill the work that God has assigned him or her to do.

It's time for us to reframe the race debate. It's not black versus white - that's the lie our enemy has presented since before Jesus walked the earth. That is the path to the dark side. Instead, the debate is dark versus light.

Christ uniquely commissioned the Church to disciple people of all nations; this means everyone! This colossal task given to the Church is not yet complete and should remain its highest priority. Jesus gave the command for the Church to work while the day is still light to fulfill the goals of evangelizing the world. Soon the night will come when no man can work.[76] If the Church continues to be distracted by racism, it will not accomplish the task Jesus gave it. Jesus finished His mission of dying for the sins of the world, so now the Church is commissioned to finish its mission of making disciples of all people, of all nations.

CHAPTER TEN

The Way Forward

"I was raised to believe that excellence is the best deterrent to racism or sexism. And that's how I operate my life."
– Oprah Winfrey

10

The Way Forward

In his book, *The Good and Beautiful Community*, James Bryan Smith pointed out a false narrative that many have maintained; "If we disagree, then we must divide."[77] He goes on to say that race, class, and doctrine have been used to separate the people of God. We have adopted this divisive false narrative and given ourselves permission to separate from those who are different than us. We are calling all people to abandon this mindset and leave it in the past. We don't have to go down the dark side! It doesn't have to be this way. It's time for us to move forward and we believe love is the foundation for our forward progress.

This takes us all being vulnerable and deciding to unite our hearts together. When people viewed our video and decided to take the time to send us an email, many of them started by saying that our video touched their hearts. So much so, that it prompted them to reach out to a total stranger and, often share personal feelings, thoughts, and emotions. They acknowledged they were inspired to change and help work towards making a change in our country.

Our hope and desire is that more people will be open to Starting Again. We must continue to work at reconciliation on a spiritual level, realizing this is a spiritual battle. It's going to require us to open our hearts to those who don't look like us and share the love. I received an email that I'll never forget. It was from a man who said he was a white supremacist. He said, "You don't know me, and I don't know you. You are a black man and I'm a white supremacist. But, after seeing your video, one thing I know for sure is that you are my brother, and I love you."

In the Light
Love leads to Forgiveness
Forgiveness leads to Unity
Unity leads to Peace

"This is the message we have heard from him and declare to you: God is light; in him there is no darkness at all. 6 If we claim to have fellowship with him and yet walk in the darkness, we lie and do not live out the truth. But if we walk in the light, as he is in the light, we have fellowship with one another, and the blood of Jesus, his Son, purifies us from all sin." 1 John 1:5-7

LOVE
Behind the greatest commandment Jesus gave to us, to love God with all of our hearts, He gave the second greatest commandment to love your neighbor as you love yourself.[78] Jesus was clear about this. Everyone equates Jesus with love. And Jesus unquestionably wanted His followers to be known for their love. He showed love in all He did and He wanted His followers to do the same. For all of us who claim to be Christians, we should regularly practice speaking the language of love. Our goal is to reflect Jesus so much that other people see Jesus in and through us. When Christians consistently model the love of Christ, the world will not only see our love, but experience loving acts too.

So the question is not should we show love, but to whom should we show it. *Who is my neighbor?* That's the question Jesus answers in the parable of the Good Samaritan. This parable teaches us that our neighbor is usually the one who we wouldn't naturally suspect. They are most likely not related to us, may not look like us, could possibly be from another country, and they usually travel in a different tribe. Pretty much, everyone is our neighbor.

This leads me to conclude that we should practice loving everyone; people who look like us and people who don't. This practice of love includes having a loving attitude towards other people and showing loving actions towards others. I believe kindness is a big part of showing love within any society. We need to be kind. I love the line from the movie, "Wonder:" "It's better to be kind than to be right." Let that sink in for a moment. Imagine how much better our society would be if everyone who claimed to be a Christian would choose to show love by being kind to everyone they encounter.

But this won't happen if we walk around with a list of people we are predisposed to dislike. Recently I was at the gas station and noticed that the attendant was fairly upset. Often when I notice this, I take it upon myself to try and cheer them up.

It doesn't Have to be this way!

When I inquired about her day she told me about an experience she had just had moments before I arrived. She had to go outside and break up a heated altercation that she thought was about to get physical. She shared this story with me while others were waiting in line behind me. It all started when two guys aggressively pulled into the gas station and parked at a pump right next to a guy minding his own business getting gas in his car. The two guys immediately started yelling at the guy pumping gas next to them. They were being very aggressive and obviously looking for a fight. It turns out that one of them thought they recognized him as a police officer who had previously arrested him. The clerk left her register and walked outside to intervene, and she heard them cursing and screaming at him. They were getting in his face and causing a scene. It turns out he wasn't a cop at all. The attendant knew this because he was a friend of hers.

He was a security guard, still in uniform, who had recently gotten off work and was trying to fill his tank and get a fountain drink. These two guys were ready to jump him because they thought he was a cop. They didn't know him or anything about him. That is ridiculous!

We should strive to be kind to people, all people, in our daily interactions. Be generous with words to encourage people. Do a spontaneous act of kindness for someone. Randomly purchase someone a cup of coffee or fountain drink. Take a moment to have a conversation with someone who you normally wouldn't. You may be surprised by how much a few minutes of your time may mean to them. Maybe even give a hug to someone who looks like they could use one. All of these things are small ways to sow the seed of love to people.

FORGIVENESS

There's nothing worse than having evil returned to you when you endeavor to do a good deed. I once woke up at 3 a.m. to travel four and a half hours to conduct a prison visit for one of our church members. The visit was scheduled for 9 a.m. and I could have forfeited my visit had I been late, so I got an early start to leave myself plenty of travel time. I arrived at the prison about an hour early and decided to take a trip back in town to burn the time. The prison was located in a small rural town about an hour southwest of Jacksonville, Florida. As a black man, I'm always extra careful when traveling through small rural towns. There have been too many bad experiences by too many black people for too long in too many small towns - so I knew to be careful and mindful of all laws.

As I was leaving the gas station and headed out of town, on my left, I happened to notice a school, a school zone sign with the flashing light, and a police officer sitting on the side of the road. I instinctively checked my speed and also noticed it was now 8:39 a.m. I had exactly 21 minutes to make it four miles down the road to the prison, so I knew I was good. As I was leaving town, I spotted another speeding sign and made careful note of the 40-mph speed limit - one can never be too careful in small towns. After I had driven a mile or so down the road, I noticed police sirens in my rearview mirror. I thought it was odd because there were no other cars around and I again looked at my speedometer and confirmed that I was only going 38 mph, a couple of miles under the limit. I wondered where the officer was going and who he was after. As he approached, I noticed that he was not going around me, so I pulled over and watched the police officer pull in behind me. I thought; "Oh, no. Here we go!"

As I was waiting for the officer to come to my car I went through the mental checklist of safe and suitable behavior for a black man getting pulled over. I kept my hands on the wheel at ten and two. I reminded myself to always address him as "sir." No quick and sudden movements. Most importantly, always, always, always inform the officer of my intent to open my glove box before reaching inside for my license and registration. Check. I was prepared.

When the officer approached my car window, he was short and to the point. "License and registration," he said, without a please. I asked him if there was a problem and why he was pulling me over. He abruptly said; "You were speeding. License and registration," nothing else. I asked for permission to get the requested items out of my glove compartment. He nodded. I retrieved the items and handed them to him. He took them and without saying another word, walked back to his car.

At this point I sat in my car thinking about what had just happened. I knew I wasn't speeding, all of my papers were up to date, and I didn't have any outstanding tickets or warrants. I wasn't afraid for what was going to happen. Instead, I was mad that I was being pulled over. Sadly, this wasn't the first time I'd been pulled over for no apparent reason, so I wasn't surprised. I accepted this as a part of "DWB" - driving while black - and hoped that I would make it to the prison on time for the scheduled visit.

When the officer returned, he curtly informed that he was giving me a citation for speeding 18 miles per hour over the speed limit, while in a school zone, and that my fine was going to be $365. To say I was shocked is more than an understatement! At this time, I was extremely upset but did my best to maintain my composure. I said: “Are you kidding me? There is no way I was speeding in the school zone!” I informed the officer that I had just turned out of the gas station and immediately noticed the school zone with him sitting there. I tried to argue that I was smart enough to know not to speed when I saw a police officer and secondly, that I didn’t have enough time to build up speed after turning out of the gas station before entering the school zone. He only responded with: “Sign the ticket.” I tried reasoning with him again, “I saw the flashing school zone light and was careful to remain under the limit . . .” He repeated himself; “Sign the ticket!” He didn’t say, “sir;” there was no “please sign the ticket,” nothing! Just cold and harsh! I went in again. I said there is no way I was speeding, this is wrong. He cut me off: “Are you refusing to sign the ticket?” I said: “Sir, this is a big pill for me to swallow!” I then tried playing the pastor card . . . “I’m a pastor from Ft. Myers, here doing a good deed of visiting one of our parishioners who is in prison.” Yada, yada, yada. He again cut me off and said, “This is the last time I’m going to tell you! If you don’t sign the ticket, I’m going to pull you out of the car, handcuff you, take you to jail and tow your car. Then you will have to pay for that too!”

I sat there in the driver’s seat of my car, staring up at him, in stunned silence. What a scam! What an abuse of power! Why the escalated threat? How rude! How unprofessional! I thought to myself, *this is obviously racially motivated*! I can’t imagine a white man would have been treated that way!

Things like this infuriate me! Sadly, I’m not the only black man who has a story like this. In fact, I’m one of the lucky ones. I was able to drive away. Do I believe that I was treated unfairly? Yes. Do I believe that the officer pulled me over because he saw I was black? Yes. Do I believe this was a case of police harassment? Yes. Was this unfair, unjust, racist? Yes. I wrestle with those thoughts, even to this day. All black people wrestle with them. However, I refuse to let the unjust treatment by this officer cause me to perceive all police officers as being the same. I refuse to become bitter or angry at all other white officers. I choose to not allow that interaction to cause me to change my belief that police, by and large, are here to serve and protect us. I choose forgiveness. This is a choice that we all must make. I choose reconciliation.

Psalm 32 is a passage of Scripture that speaks of forgiveness. That chapter teaches us how important forgiveness is and challenges us to see the blessings that come from walking in forgiveness.

Here are a few takeaways we learn from the first five verses of that chapter:

1. Blessed is the one whose sins are forgiven . . .

2. Blessed is the one who's sin the Lord does not count against him . . .

3. I was slowly dying when I failed to confess my sin . . .

4. The conviction of the Lord was constantly on me when I failed to confess my sins . . .

5. Then I acknowledged my sin and He was faithful to forgive me!

> In the Light
> LOVE leads to
> Forgiveness leads
> to Unity leads to
> PEACE

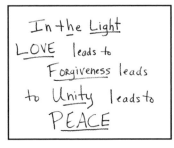

Just like we received forgiveness from God when we acknowledged our sins, so it is with other people and other races. Forgiveness is on the other side of acknowledging that we have messed up. Our opinion is that we all have played a part in the racial divide being where it is. It would do us no good to assign blame or try and decide who is more right, and who is more wrong.

Both sides have lived in the darkness of racial division. Its time for us to choose to live in the light.

This is a difficult and touchy subject when we start talking about the way forward. But we can't continue to live in the past. It's up to each of us to choose to forgive past wrongs, acknowledge that we too, at times, have been wrong, and seek forgiveness. Then we must commit to moving forward in love and unity.

I realize this is easier said than done. The hurt, pain, and hatred from the past is much too deep to let go easily. Strong feelings of bitterness and anger often emerge when we are reminded of the things done to our forefathers during slavery and the civil rights movement.

I can remember the first time I watched the "Roots" TV mini-series. I was angry with white people and didn't want anything to do with them for a while. I believe in studying history through movies, television, and books. We must look to history to understand the plight of our forefathers. We can learn from their mistakes and commit to not repeating them. However, we must not allow past sins to infuse hatred in our hearts towards the current-day descendants of those who were guilty. That's the continuation of hate. We must ask ourselves: what are we waiting on before we move on, before we let go of the hate? The way we deal with past wrongs will be noticed by our children. When we are unwilling or hesitant to come together and unite, we teach this to our children. Racism grows in their hearts and minds. Black and white parents are guilty of this. Past generations of white children have been taught to hate black people simply because of the color of their skin. Meanwhile, generations of black children have been taught to distrust white people and view them as: "The Man." It's time for forgiveness to reign.

Like most people of color who have been discriminated against, I'll admit that I wrestle with this concept of forgiveness. We all do.

But I choose to forgive those who have wronged me and wish to make amends. I even choose to forgive those who aren't seeking my forgiveness. I refuse to harbor anger, bitterness, and resentment in my heart. It does me no good. Forgiveness is a choice we all must make. I choose reconciliation. I encourage you to choose forgiveness too.

UNITY

There is a difference between *unity* and *uniformity*. Unity means that we are united or joined together as a whole.[79] Uniformity means the quality or state of being uniform.[80] Uniformity involves us all looking the same, thinking the same way, and acting the same. There's no room for individual expression when we are striving for uniformity. God created us to be diverse. He did not stamp us out from the same mold. Unlike uniformity, unity comes from diversity, not sameness.[81] That's why the goal is unity. This melting pot of people of all different shapes, sizes, and colors can all come together and form something beautiful that works well as a cohesive unit. It's time for us to realize we are indeed joined together. A common bond unites us. We are all Americans and we are all in this together.

In 2012, I had the privilege to travel to South Africa. Posted all around that mixed-race country were signs with the word; "ubuntu". When speaking to the South African People, they explain it to mean they are all united. When I returned to the States and researched the word, here's what I found. Ubuntu is a term meaning "humanity." It is often translated as *"I am because we are,"* or *"humanity towards others."* A more philosophical sense means, "the belief in a universal bond of sharing that connects all humanity."[82]

It's time for each and every one of us to do something to help bring about unity. We can't control what other people think, feel, or do. But we can control ourselves. It's time for us to take action to bridge the gap between us and our fellow man. It doesn't have to be a big undertaking. The simplest action will make a difference. We encourage you to commit to doing something to reach out to a person of another race or ethnicity with the goal of increasing your comfort level around them. We believe when you do this, other people will see you and be inspired. Then, something amazing can happen.

Here are just a few practical things you can do to get more comfortable with people who don't look like you.

Do some basic research about other cultures. It's amazing what you can learn by doing a simple Google search about other cultures.

Purposefully put yourself in situations where you will have to be around people of other races and cultures. Force yourself to be in environments where you are uncomfortable. Over time, I'm certain you will find that you will grow more comfortable in these environments. I have a few white friends who like to play basketball and found themselves gravitating to neighborhoods and gyms where they were the only white guys. Then, they soon realized they were comfortable around people of all races.

Don't be too afraid or too prideful to ask questions about other people's race and culture. Most of us are too afraid of looking stupid, so we don't ask questions about things that we don't understand. Over time, we notice we don't have much in common with these other people, so we elude them to avoid feeling awkward.

Celebrate with other people during their special events and cultural celebrations. Pay attention to the holiday traditions of others and do your research to see what they stand for. Then, ask to celebrate with a coworker or fellow church member when they observe their special days.

PEACE

People who are not Christians will not understand this message. In fact, some may find our thoughts offensive. Friends and family who don't consider their first allegiance to Jesus and His Kingdom may tell you that this message is ridiculous, that we are wasting our time striving for racial reconciliation when black people should rather be fighting against racism. Without being reconciled to God through Jesus, The Prince of Peace, we have little hope of believing that racial reconciliation can or ever will take place. They may say that we are wasting your time. They say, "Worry about your own. Take care of your own. Just stay in your lane." They consider us crazy or maybe just naive at best; however, that is a lie from the enemy. We are God's children and He wants us all to live in harmony. His will will be accomplished ultimately. Friends, we don't have to wait until heaven. We can begin to experience racial reconciliation here and now. We can't allow the world to tell us how to run the race of racial reconciliation. We can have racial peace in America.

In order for us to experience this peace we long for, we will have to ask God to search us, our minds and hearts, and to help us identify our blind spots.

Psalm 139:23-24 says: *"Search me, God, and know my heart; test me and know my anxious thoughts. See if there is any offensive way in me and lead me in the way everlasting."*

Let's examine that Scripture in light of racial reconciliation. Have you asked God to examine your heart to expose any prejudice, bigotry, racism, hate that you may have towards other races? Have you asked Him to give you a love towards people of other races and ethnicities? Ridding our hearts, minds, and lives of racism can be done, but it's going to take the power of God to expose it and eradicate it. He will do this in your life if you ask Him. God wants us to live in harmony with our brothers and sisters. Ask Him to search you.

I acknowledge that this can be awkward to do, no matter what race you are. I can remember times in the church that I grew up, we had people come and speak about race. I remember hearing sermons about racism occassionally in the churches that I have attended. I came to expect that after those services there would be a handful of white people who were going to come up to me and apologize for supposed past racial sins. They would say things like. . .

"I'm so sorry. I never knew I had those feelings in my heart towards black people."

"If I ever did or said anything to offend you, I'm really truly sorry."

"That time I asked to touch your hair, I hope that didn't offend you."

Brother, I want you to know that I love you! I love black people!

I gave those people the benefit of the doubt and trusted they meant well. God was speaking to their hearts and they wanted to respond. That's a good thing. Nonetheless, things always got really awkward.

Their motives were pure. They had some self-examination to do, which was a good thing. They wanted to acknowledge the past sins and bring them to light so that racial healing could take place. Even though it may have been a little weird, it was good to address those hidden strands of racism. (And, white people . . . I can't imagine the weight of feeling like you have to apologize for everything that anyone in your race has ever done. That's a lot of pressure).

All of us have some self-examination to do. Our goal should be to bring all the things to the light that were previously in the darkness because . . .

In the light ALL THINGS are possible

Dr. King both challenged us and gave us hope for the future in his legendary, "I Have a Dream Speech." He said many brilliant things, including this: "Now is the time to rise from the dark and desolate valley of segregation to the sunlit path of racial justice."[83] The path is lit because God has given us the grace to carry out the work of

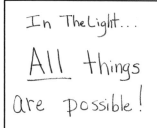

> In The Light...
> All things are possible!

bringing about racial reconciliation. God doesn't promise that it will be fast or easy. In fact, history has shown that it will be hard and long. But God does promise that He will be with us every step along the way.[84] We must be committed to persevering.

We owe it to past generations to continue to work towards equal justice for all. Dr. King said: "We will not be satisfied until justice rolls down like waters and righteousness like a mighty stream."[85]

There is a group of people who are committed to Starting Again. We saw this by the hundreds of emails we received from people who wanted to share with us pictures of their family. Most of those who sent photos shared that their family was a mixed-race family. It appears that a lot of older white people are experiencing a softening of their hearts and are becoming more open and accepting of other races. I believe this is happening because of their beautiful mixed grandchildren. Who doesn't love mixed babies?

Yet, there still is a large majority of people who, it seems, have given up on Dr. King's dream; resigned to the fact that black people and white will always run in separate, parallel races. To them, I say, we must not lose hope. Holding on to hope will enable us to live like unity has already been achieved. In so doing, we can inspire others. Little by little we will see the change we desire. So, let us not give up hope that race relations will improve. We must continue to strive to make the world better for future generations. Let us remember that Dr. King said; "I say to you today, my friends, that in spite of the difficulties and frustrations of the moment, I still have a dream."[86]

Let's Start Again

CHAPTER ELEVEN

"We – the current generation – have a moral responsibility to make the world better for future generations".

– Priscilla Chan

11

Let's Start Again

Starting again is about making things better for our kids. We need to offer them a new start, void of the racial prejudices, stereotypes, and preconceived notions that we carry. In fact, we are proposing a fresh new start for all of us. Perhaps we have traveled so far down the wrong road and gotten so far off track, that the best thing for us to do is to start all over. We have to acknowledge that we have lost our way and are way off course. Instead of fretting about our errors, let's allow ourselves the chance at a new start. Nothing is stopping us from taking this opportunity to work on improving our race relations by doing better. We have to get this right for the kids.

But this doesn't mean we have to pretend like the past never existed. After Ang and I had been married for about a year, she lost her wedding ring one evening while she was out shopping. She remembered having it at the grocery store and looking at it and admiring how beautiful it was. But, by the time she arrived home, put all the groceries away and sat on the couch to take a phone call, she was shocked to find that her ring wasn't on her finger any longer. We frantically returned to the grocery store, trying to retrace her steps. However, we were not able to find it. Fortunately, we had insurance on the ring, and minus the deductible, they were able to fully replace her beautiful wedding ring. Weeks later, after the fiasco was over, we were sitting on the couch where she had discovered the ring was gone. This time, she was admiring the beautiful replacement and beaming with joy. The jeweler was able to get her pretty much the exact same ring, cut, size and band. She was so pleased. I asked her if she was happy with the way it all turned out and she looked me dead in the eye and said, "I don't know what you are talking about! That never happened!"

Friends, unlike the lost wedding ring, we can't deny our country's atrocious history with racism, bigotry, and prejudice as though it never happened. We can't deny that we are still dealing with the effects of race as a society; economically, socially, emotionally, spiritually. We can't deny that black and brown people have a more difficult time getting ahead and becoming successful in America, even today. We hope that by now you understand that we are still facing a race problem in our country. It does us no good to try to pretend like it's not a big deal, or that it's not as bad as some may think. We can't deny that there is a problem or dismiss this as a "black people only" problem. The fuel of injustice is denial. It's hurtful to dismiss the struggle of another on the basis that "everyone struggles." That attitude lacks empathy and is thoroughly un-Christlike. Christ never dismissed a problem based on his own experience, therefore neither should we. It actually moves us further away from reconciliation when we hold these points of views.

A Facebook friend asked me a question I've been asked many times before. "Why does everything have to be about race?" I responded to him with this personal story:

When my oldest son Trey was a toddler, maybe four or five years old, he had trouble distinguishing between which grandmother we were referring to during conversations about family matters or upcoming visits. He decided to refer to them as, "Close Grandma" and "Faraway Grandma." That worked for a while, until my second son, Michael, came along. A couple of years later, when he was about three years old, he would get confused by which grandma was close and which was far away. Michael started referring to them by the most obvious differentiating trait: "Black Grandma" and "White

Grandma." This made all of us adults feel very uncomfortable for a while. We tried to get him to change this, to refer to them by some other differentiating trait: "Illinois Grandma" and "Missouri Grandma," or "Country Grandma" and "City Grandma." However, Michael wasn't having any of this and he stuck with the names he had given them - "Black Grandma" and "White Grandma." That was how he saw it and that's what stuck. It just seemed more natural to him. As a three-year-old biracial kid, he had no ill-intent in his heart. It was the simplest way of identifying the people that he interacted with and cared for the most. And still to this day, as a sixteen-year-old, he has them listed as "Black Grandma" and "White Grandma" in his phone contacts list. He's a creature of habit.

This particular issue caused Ang and I to realize we had to always acknowledge our racial differences, especially for our kids. Since that time, we have done our best to highlight the differences between the races and celebrate them. Neither race is better than the other and neither race is bad. We just have different skin colors, do some things differently, and have different traditions, routines and preferences in some areas of life! And that's OK.

We choose not to pretend like we don't see color in our family because we do. The obvious fact (noticeable even by a three-year-old) is that I'm black and Ang is white. As a black man, I notice every time I am the only minority in a room. I just do. As biracial kids, my kids notice that they are different from all the other kids. They aren't black or white. They are mixed. This reality brings with it both positives and negatives they have to live with. They've pointed out things to me that they deal with that I never would have thought or imagined they are faced with. It is what it is!

I generally believe people's heart when they say they don't see race. I know what they mean. What they are trying to communicate is that they try not to use race as a defining measure when they encounter people. That's a good thing! But the reason some people take offense to that statement is that to not see race means that we fail to see the beauty and uniqueness of different cultures, ethnicities, and races. I'm proud of my black American heritage, just like some of my friends are proud of their African heritage, or their Puerto Rican heritage, or their Jamaican heritage, or Mexican heritage. And yes, white people, you are allowed to be proud of your heritage too! We all have a right to be proud of our heritage and all that comes along with it, both good and bad. So, I'm cool with people seeing me as a big bald black man. My size, hair status, and color describe me, but they do not define me!

I'm comfortable enough to see the differences between the races, so therefore, I'm cool with talking about them and (gasp) even joking about them. God has given Ang and me a message He wants us to share. The goal is a continuing race relation dialogue that is necessary in order for us to achieve true *unity*. We have been given the opportunity to conduct race relation talks and seminars around the country in an effort to help all of us get more comfortable with this topic. Although we still have a long way to go, progress is being made one conversation at a time.

Let's start again.

We have to get comfortable talking about race in order to truly be united with each other. Let's get rid of the elephant in the room!

I've had the opportunity to play on a few championship sports teams, and one of the things that made us successful is that we were all willing to talk about issues hindering us from improving and becoming better as a team. We had to get comfortable talking about anything and everything with each other. That's the only way to truly sharpen each other and to help each other grow and improve.

I can remember one time when Ang and I were returning from a trip. We flew back into Kansas City late one Sunday evening and made our way home. After we left the airport, we wanted to get a drink, so we decided to stop at a gas station, more specifically at a

QuikTrip gas station, QT. By the way, if you don't have QTs in your area you are missing out. They are more than gas stations; they are an experience. QTs have every snack or food item you could ever want; it's all good, and you can have it quick!

Incidentally, the closest QT we saw on our way home was on the northside of Kansas City, in an area that is racially diverse. When we pulled in, we immediately noticed a lot of young black people there. Some were lingering by their cars talking. Some were at the gas pumps just sitting there, some were inside the store getting drinks, and many were standing outside the front door just talking. There were a lot of black kids hanging out at this QT around 11p.m. It seemed weird, not wrong, just weird. They weren't doing anything they shouldn't be doing, but I wasn't used to seeing this many people, of any race, just hanging out at any QT, and I've been to a lot of them. Ang and I walked in and she headed to the bathroom while I went to get our drinks. At the drink station I asked a couple of the guys what was going on. They explained they usually go skating on Sunday nights and then come to this QT when they are done just to chill. Pretty cool. I loved hearing this. It was awesome seeing this many young black people hanging out, fellowshipping after a night of good clean fun. They don't talk about this on the news.

Ang finished in the bathroom and we met at the register, quickly paid for our drinks and headed to our car. Up to this point, neither of us had commented on this experience. I wasn't sure what Ang was thinking, but I was certain that she, like I, had noticed all the black people. She's occasionally in environments where she is the only white person and she is cool with that. However, she was aware she stood out from the rest of the people there that night.

Once we were on our way, Ang shared with me what was going through her mind. She explained how the experience got her thinking about the awkward state of race relations in our country. She went on to explain the thoughts that went through her mind while she was in the store. She said, "I was not nervous or scared about being the only white person in the store. I never felt threatened or intimidated in any way, but it was just awkward."

Angie went on, "You know how when you've been a part of a class or group for something for long enough that you should know everyone's name, but you haven't ever learned them? And then, you run into someone outside of the group and there is an awkward exchange? You hope that you can either avoid being noticed by them or that, if you have to speak, the issue of whether or not you know their name doesn't come up." She said, "That's how I felt tonight, I had an internal monologue that went like this: I know that these people all seem perfectly good and nice and respectable. I'm not uncomfortable being here around them, but I bet that they think that I am uncomfortable. So, do I say something clever or engaging in an effort to show that I am in fact cool with being a white person in a big group of black people? Or, do I just go about my business, get my drink, and mind my own business? It was like that. Just awkward. I'm kind of sad because it's 2018 and we should be farther along in our race relationships so that we don't have to overthink all this silliness. If that had been a group of white young adults, I wouldn't have had the monologue in my head. I would have simply either gotten my drink and left or chosen to speak to someone if I felt like it. I would not have questioned my thought process nor that of the group of people in the store."

Angie continued to say: "This is the state of race relations in America. We should be more comfortable interacting with each other, but we aren't." We should make sure we are learning each other's names (so to speak) so that when we interact with each other, it's not so awkward. We have to do a better job of getting into other people's worlds so that we are more comfortable interacting with each other.

For US

Starting again is about us Christians making sure that other people and future generations have the opportunity to be exposed to the light. Light shines on darkness to drive it out.[87] Christians are called to go into the world and find darkness so that we can be the light that shines on it. Jesus told us to let our light shine before people so they can see our good deeds, and this will bring glory to the Father.[88] Racism, hate, prejudice, and bigotry can all be overcome when Christians begin living and loving like Christ and letting our light shine so that the world can see it. Let us choose forgiveness and peace.

Unity can happen when we choose to give other people the benefit of the doubt. When the benefit of the doubt is given, dialogue remains open. We need open, face to face, personal dialogue between individuals. The media and news outlets are reporting on racial issues and when they do, quite often Facebook and Twitter are filled with people giving their opinions and making comments about racism. But people are not talking – they are arguing. It seems as though face to face, cordial and civil dialogue has taken a back seat to arguing and trolling. People appear to be bolder on social media or behind the keys of their keyboard than they are face to face.

Cordial friendly dialogue where people can express their feelings and beliefs is what we are after. As Christians, we should help facilitate dialogue. We are the ones who can help frame the dialogue from a Biblical perspective. Remember, we are the ones who are called to have a ministry of reconciliation. When we remember that our goal is unity, we will create environments where both sides feel they have freedom to express their points of view, without being judged, ridiculed, or attacked.

Let me offer this to my white brothers and sisters. Please remember, being in the majority, you have a different vantage point than those of us who are always in the minority class. We see things differently because we have different experiences to pull from. As a sixth grader, I was the only black kid to walk into my elementary school every day. I doubt many of you reading this book have ever been in a situation where you were the only white person, anywhere (let alone attending school or working every day in that environment). You would probably have some stories to share about your experiences. Think about how you might feel if that was your reality. Black people have some stories to tell. When they are willing to share about their experiences and openly talk about their feelings on race relations, that's a good thing. If they are willing to describe an incident where they were offended or wronged in the past, it means they are open to taking steps toward repairing the relationship. It means they are willing to try to let you into their world because a relationship with you is important to them. It means they are opening themselves up for dialogue. And that is always a good thing.

Let's start a dialogue with each other that will help us seek to understand our fellow man. The goal is to bring people together.

We won't have an open and honest dialogue until we have built durable and lasting relationships with people. They have to trust what we say. It will require us demonstrating that our motives are pure, and we are sincere about coming together. We need unity in our communities, not arguments, hate, or division. We need to become intentional about building relationships that cross race and culture.

One of my favorite Denzel Washington movies is "Remember the Titans." (Random question, had I only said Denzel, would you have immediately known who I was referring to? I think Denzel is one of those one-name people like Oprah, De Niro, Obama.) Back to the story, "Remember the Titans" is based on actual events in 1971 in Alexandria, Virginia. This is the story of a black football coach and his high school team. Coach Herman Boone was given the difficult task of becoming head coach of a recently desegregated school's football team while replacing the highly successful white coach who remained on the coaching staff, now as a subordinate. As you can imagine, tension was high, and racism was blatant. This was a recipe for disaster. However, the team becomes the unifying symbol for the community as the boys and the adults learn to depend on and trust each other.[89] Trust among the team was developed because Coach Boone forced the team to start interacting with each other. He told them to spend time each day with a teammate of a different race. He wanted them to learn about that teammate and his family, to figure out their likes and dislikes. It was great advice. This interaction led to trust, trust led to unity, and the unity brought this team together to have a perfect record for that football season. The success of the football team caused their small community in Virginia to accept the integration and become more kind to people of different races. The good advice from Coach Boone is good advice for us today. We should make it a priority to spend time on a regular basis with people who don't look like us. All people should do this, and Christians should lead the way in modeling this.

There seems to be a void of people seeking unity in the Christian world, with many believers choosing to be silent and unwilling to engage in conversation that may bring about racial reconciliation. Many Christians are afraid of opening their mouth and saying something wrong, so they keep silent and say nothing. The rise of political correctness and the fear of broaching politically correct culture has caused many Christians to stay on the sidelines on this issue. If this is you, can I encourage you with the words that the Apostle Paul gave to his young protege Timothy when he was encouraging him to step up and be a leader? He told him God has not given him the spirit of fear, but of power and of love and of a sound mind.[90] Another translation uses the word *timidity* instead of *fear.*[91] God doesn't want His followers to be timid and silent on this issue. When we are led by His spirit and walk in love, we don't have to fear saying the wrong thing. We can walk in boldness knowing that we are delivering the message He has given us. God wants us to walk in power while delivering His message of love, forgiveness, unity, and peace!

Don't take the bait

We must not be Christians who miss opportunities to influence others by taking the bait of arguing our points of view. To truly listen to the experience of another person requires us to focus on listening and not on formulating a rebuttal. Too often we don't listen to what others are saying because we are too busy formulating our rebuttal. This is quite common in this day and age given the highly volatile political climate we have in America. By engaging in political arguments, I've seen too many Christians end up offending the very people we are called to reach. This is a mistake.

My family tried to address this issue during the election season in a video we posted on Facebook, called "Civility." This video shows my family making a series of statements encouraging people to be civil. It was well received as it had over 56,000 views and was shared over 1,100 times on Facebook. Here's the script:

> *This shouldn't have to be said...*
> *But unfortunately, it has to be.*
>
> *People – Be civil!*
>
> *Whatever happened to civility?*
> *What does it mean to be civil?*
> *According to dictionary.com, the definition of civility is...*
> *"Courtesy." "Politeness." "A polite action or expression."*
>
> *We don't have enough civility in America today!*
> *We have a lot of fighting, arguing, and rudeness.*
> *But not enough civility!*
>
> *I know the election season presents us with two different choices for America's future...*
> *Do you trust the Democratic plan or Republican plan?*
> *Right or Left*
> *Red or Blue*
>
> *I hear some people say, "I don't care who you vote for, just vote."*

Well, I DO CARE WHO YOU VOTE FOR.

And, I'm honest enough to say it.
Because my candidate represents the future of America that I envision!
So, I do hope that you vote the way I vote.
But, even if you don't.
I'm still gonna be polite to you.
I'm still gonna respect you.
I'm not gonna call you names.
I'm not gonna question love for America
I still choose to love you.

It's really pretty simple . . .
We learned all this in kindergarten.

That's civility.

Can we all agree that it's time for us to be civil?
Even when we disagree . . . be civil!
When someone votes differently . . . be civil!
If you are red or if you are blue . . . be civil!

Sending bombs in the mail to political opponents?
NOT OK!
Hating on and protesting gay people?
NOT OK!
Screaming at the wife of a fallen 9/11 police officer?
NOT OK!
Shooting up churches and other public places filled with people you may not like or agree with?
NOT OK!
Disrespecting the First Lady?
Also, NOT OK!

Let's choose civility!
Let's Start Again! [92]

We need dialogue. People should feel safe enough to share their opinions, and Christians should be the ones leading and facilitating this dialogue. Instead, the people facilitating the dialogue are not the ones intent on bringing light into the world. They are doing some good by starting dialogue for open discussion on racism, injustice, prejudice, bigotry, etc. However, I feel they allow the discussion to go too far, allowing people to speak, "their truth." They often end up making assertions that do more to divide us than unite us. White fragility, white women's tears, and white guilt are all controversial topics that were birthed from open dialogue forums about racism.

Howard Shultz, longtime CEO and chairman of Starbucks, shared about what his company is doing to address racism and social injustice in his book, *From the Ground UP*. Starbucks hosted forums where employees could speak freely about race relations in the U.S. These were so productive that they decided to host open forums in their coffee shops where people of all backgrounds could come together and discuss race issues. Shultz said: "We have to nurture a culture of respectful discussion where this type of conversation could exist. If we create a history of people speaking freely at open forums, even if people disagree with each other or feel angry about a discussion matter, the tone can stay civil."[93]

We need discussion. Someone has to moderate these discussions. That's why Christians need to enter the discussion and seek to see both sides. Christians have to show that people can trust us to show love when they choose to present their opinions and views. It doesn't mean that we have to agree with everything everyone says. But we have to be trusted to listen well and respond in a non-judgmental and loving ways. We can still be the holders of truth, but we have to allow room for people to express their opinions in safe spaces, while they are on their journey to arrive at truth.

In addition, even when we find we can't reach common ground, Christians should be respectful of all people. This includes people we disagree with and people we may never see eye to eye with.

Figuring out how to do this is the tricky part. There are two proverbs in the Bible that have given me wisdom in this area. Proverbs 26:4 says, "Do not answer a fool according to his folly, or you yourself will be just like him." But the very next verse, Proverbs 26:5 seems to suggest the opposite. It says, "answer a fool according to his folly, or he will be wise in his own eyes." This may seem a little confusing; are we to be quiet while talking to a foolish person or do we set the record straight and put them in their place? (The latter usually gets my vote) But, I've found this to mean that sometimes we are to be quiet and sometimes we are to speak up. When a person says something to reveal foolish thinking, the wise person will recognize the foolishness and avoid engagement in any meaningful way. When there is no common ground to be found, sometimes the best thing to do, so that no lasting damage is done, is just walk away and let the issue die. Let us be reminded of what Howard Shultz said in his book, "even if people disagree, the tone should stay civil." This isn't always easy, but it is worth it if we plan to Start Again.

The goal is for us to bring light into the darkness. In his book, *Follow Me*, David Platt asks the question. "How will we spread God's glory among all people?" We do this by remembering the eternal purpose of God, which is to save people through Christ. Our purpose is to spend our lives working to impact every person of every nation, tribe and tongue. We must abandon ourselves to His will and to be His witness in and to the world.[94] We can't do this by arguing and fighting with each other. Jesus told believers this 2,000 years ago - and it still applies to us today. The message from Jesus needs to continue to be declared to all the world. God is light! Christians are given the task of showing this to the world. In spite of all the hatred, bigotry, and racism we see, we have to be the ones who take on the task of demonstrating this truth to the world. When we walk in the light, like Jesus taught us to, we can have true fellowship with each other. We can model this for the rest of the world to see.

We can do it. We must do it. For our kids and for each other -
Let's Start Again!

End Notes

[1] https://en.wikipedia.org/wiki/2016_shooting_of_Dallas_police_officers

[2]www.archives.gov/exhibits/featured-documents/emancipation-proclamation

[3] 2 Corinthians 5:18 paraphrased.

[4] 2 Corinthians 5:11-14 The Message version paraphrased.

[5] https://www.americamagazine.org/politics-society/2017/11/20/racism-sickness-soul-can-jesuit-spirituality-help-us-heal

[6] https://billygrahamlibrary.org/billy-graham-racism/

[7] https://www.wired.com/2016/07/physical-damage-racism-inflicts-brain-body/

[8] "Blackish" television show Season 1, Episode 9.

[9] Fox News television interview, 2019.

[10] Lance Selfa, "Slavery and the Origins of Racism," International Socialist Review, Issue 26 (November-December, 2002): 1-2, accessed July 9, 2018.

[11] David Brion Davis, *The Problem of Slavery in the Age of Emancipation* (New York: Knopf Doubleday Publishing Group, 2014).

[12] John 10:10a (NIV) "The thief comes only to steal and kill and destroy."

[13] According to the story in John 4 with Jesus and the Woman of Samaria.

[14] Andrew E. Hill and John H. Walton, *A Survey of the New Testament.* (Grand Rapids, MI: Zondervan, 2012).

[15] According to the story in Luke 10:25-37, the parable of the Good Samaritan.

[16] John 10:27 (NIV), "My sheep listen to my voice; I know them, and they follow me."

[17] 2 Chronicles 15:2b (NIV), "The Lord is with you when you are with him. If you seek him, he will be found by you, but if you forsake him, he will forsake you."

[18] Covey, Stephen R. *The 7 Habits of Highly Effective People: Powerful Lessons in Personal Change*. (New York: Free, 2004).

[19] Quick MBA Management, Knowledge to power your business.

[20] Larry R. Morrison, "The Religious Defense of American Slavery Before 1830," The Journal of Religious Thought, Kings College online journal. Accessed 7/13/18. https://www.kingscollege.net/gbrodie/.pdf

[21] Bill O'Reilly and Martin Dugard, *Killing England: The Brutal Struggle for American Independence* (New York, NY: Henry Holt and Co., 2017), 147.

[22] https://en.wikipedia.org/wiki/Institutional_racism

[23] Terry Jones, "Institutional Racism in the United States" Social Work Journal, Volume 19, No. 2 (March 1974): pp. 218-225, accessed September 17, 2019.

[24] According to dictionary.com

[25] https://en.wikipedia.org/wiki/Urban_decay

[26] Video on Google from December 15, 2014.

[27] Gonzalez, Sandra (January 29, 2019). "Empire star Jussie Smollett attacked in possible hate crime". CNN. Atlanta: Turner Broadcasting System.

[28] Psalm 5:4 (ESV).

[29] James 1:13-16 (ESV), "Let no one say when he is tempted, 'I am being tempted by God,' for God cannot be tempted with evil, and he himself tempts no one. But each person is tempted when he is lured and enticed by his own desire. Then desire when it has conceived gives birth to sin, and sin when it is fully grown brings forth death. Do not be deceived, my beloved brothers."

[30] Alister E. McGrath, ed. *The Christian Theology Reader* 5th Edition (Malden, MA: Wiley-Blackwell, 2016). 356.

[31] www.bbc.com/news/newsbeat-44209141

[32] Roc Nation is an American entertainment company founded by Jay-Z in 2008.

[33] GOOD Music was founded in 2004 by Kanye West.

[34] Bad Boy is an American record label founded in 1993 by Sean Combs.

[35] Aftermath Entertainment is an American record label founded by hip hop producer and rapper Dr. Dre.

[36] Doggy Style Records (formerly known as Dogghouse Records) is an American record label founded by rapper Snoop Dogg in 1995.

[37] Def Jam Recordings is the hip-hop music label co-founded by Russell Wendell Simmons.

[38] Strange Music is an American independent record label specializing in hip hop music and founded by Tech N9ne and Travis O'Guin in 1999.

[39] No Limit Records was an American record label founded by rapper, entrepreneur and CEO Percy "Master P" Miller.

[40] http://harvardpolitics.com/books-arts/politics-race-rap/

[41] Proverbs 12:18 (NIV).

[42] Ephesians 6:12-13 (NIV), "For our struggle is not against flesh and blood, but against the rulers, against the authorities, against the powers of this dark world and against the spiritual forces of evil in the heavenly realms. Therefore, put on the full armor of God, so that when the day of evil comes, you may be able to stand your ground, and after you have done everything, to stand."

[43] Walter C. Kaiser, *Mission in the Old Testament: Israel as a Light to the Nations*. (Grand Rapids, MI: Baker Books, 2000), 48.

[44] John V. York, *Missions in the Age of the Spirit* (Springfield, MO: Logion, 2000), 796 Kindle.

[45] John 10:10 (NIV), "The thief comes only to steal and kill and destroy; I have come that they may have life, and have it to the full.

[46] R. Scott Rodin, The Steward Leader: Transforming People, Organizations and Communities. (Downers Grove, IL: InterVarsity Press, 2010), 45-46.

[47] Rodin, 46.

[48] Rodin, 46.

[49] Colossians 1:16 (NIV), "For in him all things were created: things in heaven and on earth, visible and invisible, whether thrones or powers or

rulers or authorities; all things have been created through him and for him."

[50] Romans 3:23 (NIV), "For all have sinned and fall short of the glory of God."

[51] Romans 6:23 (NIV), "For the wages of sin is death, but the gift of God is eternal life in[a] Christ Jesus our Lord."

[52] John 3:16 (NIV), "For God so loved the world that he gave his one and only Son, that whoever believes in him shall not perish but have eternal life."

[53] Romans 10:9-10 (NIV), "If you declare with your mouth, Jesus is Lord, and believe in your heart that God raised him from the dead, you will be saved. For it is with your heart that you believe and are justified, and it is with your mouth that you profess your faith and are saved.

[54] Adapted from *The Star Thrower*, by Loren Eiseley (1907–1977).

[55] "Luv Is a Verb" lyrics. Songwriters: George Cocchini / Mark Heimemann / Toby Mckeehan.

[56] "The RS 500 Greatest Songs of All Time." rollingstone.com. 2004-12-09.

[57] Jeremiah 17:9 (New Living Translation). "The human heart is the most deceitful of all things, and desperately wicked. Who really knows how bad it is?"

[58] McIntosh, G.L. & Rima, S. D. (2007). *Overcoming the Dark Side of Leadership: How to Become an Effective Leader by Confronting Potential Failures.* Grand Rapids, MI: Baker Books.

[59] Romans 3:23 (NIV), "For all have sinned and fall short of the glory of God."

[60] McIntosh and Rima. *Overcoming the Dark Side of Leadership.* (Chapter 15)

[61] 1 John 1:5-7 (NIV)

[62] Luke 6:45 (Contemporary English Version)

[63] Matthew 28:19 (NIV), "Therefore go and make disciples of all nations, baptizing them in the name of the Father and of the Son and of the Holy Spirit."

[64] Harvey Cox, *Fire from Heaven: The Rise of Pentecostal Spirituality and the Reshaping of Religion in the Twenty-first Century.* (Cambridge, MA: Da

Capo Press, 1995), 48-64.

[65] Erik J. Hjalmeby, “A Rhetorical History of Race Relations in the Early Pentecostal Movement, 1906-1916,” Baylor University, August 2007.

[66] Daniel K. Norris, “How Azusa Street Exposed – and Overturned Racism in the Church,” Charisma News: October 11, 2016.

[67] Matthew 28:19-20 (NIV) ,“Therefore go and make disciples of all nations, baptizing them in the name of the Father and of the Son and of the Holy Spirit, and teaching them to obey everything I have commanded you. And surely I am with you always, to the very end of the age.”

[68] Ernest Cleo Grant II, “Whitewashed Christianity,” The Witness: October 25, 2016.

[69] The Leviathan is mentioned five times in Scripture: Job 3:8, Job 40:15–41:26, Psalm 74:13–23, Psalm 104:26, and Isaiah 27:1.

[70] Grant II, “Whitewashed Christianity.”

[71] Psalms 133:1 (English Standard Version)

[72] Joel 2:32a (NIV), “And everyone who calls on the name of the LORD will be saved”

[73] Malachi 2:10a (English Standard Version)

[74] Galatians 3:28 (English Standard Version)

[75] Revelations 7:9-10 (English Standard Version)

[76] James 9:4 (English Standard Version)

[77] James Bryan Smith. *The Good and Beautiful Community.* (InterVarsity Press: Downers Grove, IL. 2010)

[78] Matthew 22:38-39 (NIV), “This is the first and greatest commandment. And the second is like it: ‘Love your neighbor as yourself’”.

[79] According to dictionary.com.

[80] According to Merriam-Webster Dictionary.

[81] Elisabeth Elliot. *The Path of Loneliness: Finding Your Way Through the Wilderness to God.* (Revell: Grand Rapids, MI. 1998, 2001).

[82] https://en.m.wikipedia.org/wiki/Ubuntu_philosophy.

[83] Excerpt from MLK Speech, "I Have a Dream . . ." (Copyright 1963, Martin Luther King, JR.) Speech by the Rev. Martin Luther King, Jr. at the "March on Washington."

[84] 1 Kings 8:57 (KJV) The LORD our God be with us, as he was with our fathers: let him not leave us, nor forsake us.

[85] Excerpt from MLK Speech, "I HAVE A DREAM ..."

[86] Excerpt from MLK Speech, "I HAVE A DREAM ..."

[87] John 1:5 (Contemporary English Version), "The light keeps shining in the dark, and darkness has never put it out."

[88] Matthew 5:16 (NIV), "In the same way, let your light shine before others, that they may see your good deeds and glorify your Father in heaven."

[89] https://www.imdb.com/title/tt0210945/plotsummary

[90] 2 Timothy 1:7 (NKJV), "For God has not given us a spirit of fear, but of power and of love and of a sound mind."

[91] 2 Timothy 1:7 (New American Standard Bible), "For God has not given us a spirit of timidity, but of power and love and discipline."

[92] You can view the video on Facebook using the hashtag, #choosecivility

[93] Howard Schultz, *From the Ground Up* (New York, NY: Random House, 2019).

[94] David Platt, *Follow Me* (Carol Stream, Illinois: Tyndale House Publishers, 2013).